MW00526529

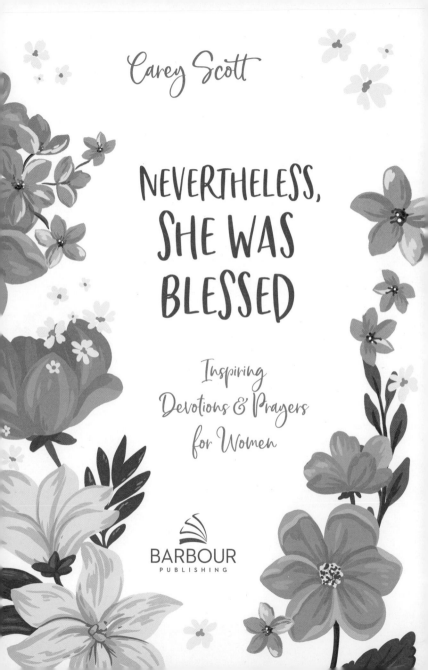

Carey Scott

NEVERTHELESS, SHE WAS BLESSED

Inspiring Devotions & Prayers for Women

BARBOUR
PUBLISHING

Published by Barbour Publishing, Inc., 1810 Barbour Drive, Uhrichsville, Ohio 44683, www.barbourbooks.com

Our mission is to inspire the world with the life-changing message of the Bible.

Printed in China.

NEVERTHELESS, YOU ARE BLESSED!

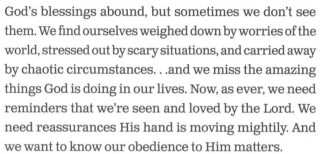

God's blessings abound, but sometimes we don't see them. We find ourselves weighed down by worries of the world, stressed out by scary situations, and carried away by chaotic circumstances. . .and we miss the amazing things God is doing in our lives. Now, as ever, we need reminders that we're seen and loved by the Lord. We need reassurances His hand is moving mightily. And we want to know our obedience to Him matters.

Let this book open your eyes and prepare your heart to recognize the beautiful and powerful gifts from God present in your life right now. Through its pages, let Him redirect your attention from earthly battles to eternal blessings. And be encouraged that God is alive and active. You may be struggling today; nevertheless you are blessed!

YOU CAN'T EARN IT

*For by grace you have been saved by faith. Nothing
you did could ever earn this salvation, for it was the
love gift from God that brought us to Christ! So no
one will ever be able to boast, for salvation is never
a reward for good works or human striving.*

EPHESIANS 2:8–9 TPT

What a blessing to realize your salvation has nothing to do with
how good you are or how much you do. You can't earn it. And
you cannot pay for it. Instead, recognize it as a gift from God
through His Son, Jesus. As women, we are used to being doers.
We are hard workers who juggle a million different things at
once. From managing a home to managing a staff, our to-do
lists are lengthy and weighty. But when it comes to faith, it's not
about striving or organization. It's about responding to God's
gift of salvation by embracing His truth.

• •

*Dear God, thank You that salvation is a gift and not something
I must work for. In the name of Jesus I pray. Amen.*

4

FOLLOWING GOD'S WAYS

What delight comes to the one who follows God's ways!
He won't walk in step with the wicked, nor share the
sinner's way, nor be found sitting in the scorner's seat.
PSALM 1:1 TPT

Every time you choose God's way over the world's way, that intentional choice sets you up for a blessing. Not only does it bring you closer to God, but it puts more distance between you and the enemy's plans. It builds a barrier between you and the wicked. And it keeps you focused on the good things God is doing in your life. Even when the journey takes you through the valley, your spirit will be in step with His as He guides you safely through. You will feel delighted by your courage and confident to stay committed to the Lord's way, not tempted by the world's.

• •

Dear God, bless me with the courage to always choose Your
way over anything the world offers. There is no substitute
for Your goodness! In the name of Jesus I pray. Amen.

AT THE END OF YOUR ROPE

*"You're blessed when you're at the end of your rope.
With less of you there is more of God and his rule."*
MATTHEW 5:3 MSG

When was the last time you were at the end of your rope? We all find ourselves there at times, often more than we'd like. We've never thought of it as a good place to be. It's never a positive, right? Being at the end of our rope is usually a negative. But today's scripture challenges us to see it another way. Consider that when you get to that place, it means there's more room for God to manifest in your situation. When you give up control, it allows Him to step in. What a huge blessing, if you really think about it!

. . . .

Dear God, thank You for shifting my perspective to see the blessing of being at the end of my rope. I know it's a good place because less of me means more of You, and that's always the best way. In the name of Jesus I pray. Amen.

6

DEEPLY ROOTED

He will be standing firm like a flourishing tree planted by God's design, deeply rooted by the brooks of bliss, bearing fruit in every season of life. He is never dry, never fainting, ever blessed, ever prosperous.
PSALM 1:3 TPT

Deeply rooted, ever blessed. . .this is what it's like when you connect your life to God's. When you embrace who He is and grow in your relationship with Him, it deepens your roots of faith and holds you steady when the storms come. And they will. Chances are they already have. What's more, the time spent cultivating community with the Lord allows you to be a fruit bearer regardless of what's happening in your life. You will always see the silver lining. You will have peace and joy even in the messiest times. And you'll find a deep desire to let Him guide your life, blessing you along the way.

* *

Dear God, it's a blessing to be deeply rooted in You. Help me flourish as I invest in our relationship. I want to know You more! In the name of Jesus I pray. Amen.

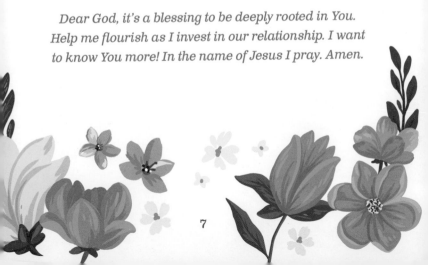

7

WHO IS MOST DEAR?

"You're blessed when you feel you've lost what is most dear to you. Only then can you be embraced by the One most dear to you."
MATTHEW 5:4 MSG

This verse is a powerful challenge to see the difference between *what* is most important and *who* is most important in your life. Too often we blur the lines and cannot distinguish the difference. Maybe what's most dear to you right now is your career or your health or your finances. It's become almost an automatic decision to place that above everything else in your life, including God. But when what is most dear is taken from us—for whatever reason—clarity eventually comes. It's faith that opens our eyes to realize these idols have replaced the Lord. And when you see it, be blessed as you realign priorities.

* *

Dear God, help me keep You above all else in my life. In the name of Jesus I pray. Amen.

8

THE BATTLE FOR CONTENTMENT

"You're blessed when you're content with just who you are—
no more, no less. That's the moment you find yourselves
proud owners of everything that can't be bought."

MATTHEW 5:5 MSG

Oh friend, the struggle we face to be content with who we are is one we've faced for years. For many of us, it's a battle we have waged since childhood. And while we know there's a blessing attached to contentment, we grapple in our strength to find it. We try to will it to be. But at the end of the day, we're tangled in the same insecurities, worried we'll never be enough. It's when we involve God that we find peace with who we are. Let Him bless you with a love for yourself that's eluded you too long. You are not perfect, but the truth is you're not supposed to be. God made you with great intention and delights in His creation.

. . . .

Dear God, bless me with self-assurance anchored
in You. In the name of Jesus I pray. Amen.

AN APPETITE FOR GOD

"You're blessed when you've worked up a good appetite for God. He's food and drink in the best meal you'll ever eat."

MATTHEW 5:6 MSG

How do you work up a good appetite for God? Think about what food you like the most. Do you crave it? Do you think about it? Maybe you find recipes to make for your friends and family, working them into your meal planning on the regular. Your favorite restaurants probably serve that food, and you know the exact aisle at your local grocery store to find it in. And when you want to celebrate or you need comfort, you know the perfect eats to satisfy. Friend, let God be a destination just like your favorite food. Think about Him throughout your day and make time to invest in your relationship together. Let Him be your craving and the One who satisfies. You will be blessed when you seek God with all your heart.

. . . .

Dear God, help me crave You more than anything else in the world. In the name of Jesus I pray. Amen.

THE TOOL OF TENDER MERCY

"How blessed you are when you demonstrate tender mercy! For tender mercy will be demonstrated to you."

MATTHEW 5:7 TPT

Sometimes people see mercy as a wimpy characteristic to have. They think it means you are weak or a wet noodle. What they are missing is the truth that tender mercy is a powerful tool in the hands of a believer. To be a person of compassion takes courage. You must have a certain level of confidence to be kind. When people are generous, it's often an indicator of their commitment to following God's will. And when you choose to wield this powerful tool for the kingdom, you will be blessed in meaningful ways. As a matter of fact, scripture says that mercy will be given back to you. It's a win-win.

. . . .

Dear God, thank You for affirming that mercy is weighty and not wimpy. And thank You for the promise of blessing back. In the name of Jesus I pray. Amen.

11

YOUR INSIDE WORLD

*"You're blessed when you get your inside
world—your mind and heart—put right.
Then you can see God in the outside world."*
MATTHEW 5:8 MSG

It all starts on the inside, doesn't it? We live out of what we think, and we act out of what we feel. So if our minds are filled with anger and unforgiveness, that's how we will relate to the world. If we allow our insecurities to run rampant, we will never feel content or safe. When we decide we're better than others, our words will reflect that prideful attitude. But getting our inside world put right requires God's help. Alone, we can't fix our hearts or minds. It's the Lord who blesses us through His promises—promises that still our spirits and give us hope. When we anchor our faith there, we will be able to radiate those precious beliefs to the outside world and bless others at the same time.

*Dear God, I need You to put my mind and
heart right. Bless me so I can bless others.
In the name of Jesus I pray. Amen.*

12

SHOW THEM HOW
TO COOPERATE

"You're blessed when you can show people how to cooperate instead of compete or fight. That's when you discover who you really are, and your place in God's family."
MATTHEW 5:9 MSG

Let today's verse challenge you to be a leader who stands up for what is right. Be encouraged to be the kind of woman who brings diplomacy into the mix. Help others see the value in replacing chaos with cooperation. We live in a dog-eat-dog world where we learn to compete with one another at an early age. We learn to fight to get what we want. But living this way only creates animosity toward one another. The Lord says if you can help others see the value in working together, you will be blessed by it. They will be blessed by it. And it will solidify your identity in the faith.

. . . .

Dear God, I know You appreciate the peacemaker.
Give me the insight and inspiration to be one.
In the name of Jesus I pray. Amen.

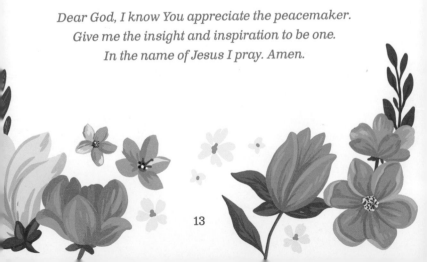

BLESSED BY PERSECUTION

"You're blessed when your commitment to God provokes persecution. The persecution drives you even deeper into God's kingdom. Not only that—count yourselves blessed every time people put you down or throw you out or speak lies about you to discredit me. What it means is that the truth is too close for comfort and they are uncomfortable."
MATTHEW 5:10–11 MSG

When you're unashamedly bold in your belief, it will delight the Lord. It's the kind of faith that changes lives. In the same vein, it's also the kind of faith that provokes persecution. Many times, when we feel criticized or judged, we retreat. We shut our mouths. But God is offering a different perspective once again. He puts a premium on shaking people out of their comfort zone because it challenges their thinking and opens them up to truth. So don't shy away from standing firm in your belief. Be confident as you share your love of God. And know every time persecution results from it, you're blessed.

. . . .

*Dear God, help me see persecution as a blessing.
In the name of Jesus I pray. Amen.*

THE BLESSING OF A FRESH START

Count yourself lucky, how happy you must be—you get a fresh start, your slate's wiped clean. Count yourself lucky—GOD holds nothing against you and you're holding nothing back from him.

PSALM 32:1-2 MSG

Once you give your life to the Lord, amazing things happen. One of the most notable is a fresh start. Who wouldn't want their messy slate of failures and shortcomings wiped clean? Think of all the choices you wish you hadn't made. Remember the decisions that led you to dark places. We've all compromised our morals and crossed boundaries we said we never would. But friend, your faith ensures that none of this is held against you. It is forgiven once and for all. You are blessed with a clean slate, forever unsoiled because of Jesus. In God's eyes, you are spotless. From this point forward, He sees you through the blood of His Son, who took away every sin—past, present, future—on the cross.

. . . .

Dear God, I'm so grateful for a fresh start. Thank You for Your grace. In the name of Jesus I pray. Amen.

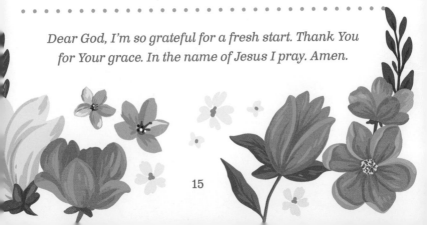

UNINTIMIDATED

Why would anyone harm you if you eagerly do good? Even if you should suffer for doing what is right, you will receive a blessing. Don't let them frighten you. Don't be intimidated.
1 PETER 3:13–14 VOICE

Ask God to bless you with confidence to choose the right things. Ask for courage to stand strong in the face of criticism and do what glorifies His name. This isn't always the popular stance to take, because it often goes against the world's ways. What God wants for you and what society wants for you are vastly different. But when you draw a hard line in the sand and remain committed to the Lord, scripture says you'll receive a blessing. So don't shy away from asking God to strengthen you to do what is respectful. Whenever weakness creeps in, let Him know you need help. Others will try to intimidate you and scare you out of being faithful, but God will bless you with resolve to choose Him.

. . . .

Dear God, I will stand firm in my faith and do the right thing with Your help. In the name of Jesus I pray. Amen.

COMING CLEAN TO GOD

*Then I let it all out; I said, "I'll come clean about
my failures to GOD." Suddenly the pressure was
gone—my guilt dissolved, my sin disappeared.*

PSALM 32:5 MSG

Anything kept tucked away in the dark is the devil's playground.
Any secrets you're hiding, any habits you're covering, and any
sin you're concealing gives the enemy a foothold in your life.
It's his way in to discourage you and destroy what you hold
dear. Are you struggling with shame and guilt and pressure
to be perfect? If so, blame the enemy. Those are some of the
most powerful arrows in his quiver. But God has thought of
everything. When you come clean to Him, He shines a light,
and the enemy's arrows lose power. They become ineffective
because God is completely effective. And He will bless you with
freedom to live and love with fervor.

• •

*Dear God, You know the places where I struggle with
guilt and shame. Shine Your light to reveal so You
can heal. In the name of Jesus I pray. Amen.*

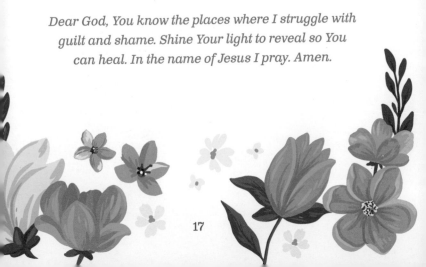

17

HAPPINESS IS POSSIBLE

Happy is the person who can hold up under the trials of life. At the right time, he'll know God's sweet approval and will be crowned with life. As God has promised, the crown awaits all who love Him.

JAMES 1:12 VOICE

Today's scripture tells us there is a connection between happiness and weathering the storms of life. Many of us have been knocked down by hardship. We lost a marriage. We lost someone dear to a ruthless disease. We lost our jobs or filed bankruptcy. We suffered broken relationships. We watched a child take the wrong path. And rather than cling to the Lord, we buckled under the pressure of carrying the hardship ourselves. But we can choose differently. Next time the storms hit, go right to God for help. Let Him strengthen and bless you so you're able to find joy even in the mess.

. . . .

Dear God, help me stand strong in life's tough battles. And bless me with happiness and Your approval as I do. In the name of Jesus I pray. Amen.

YOUR HIDING PLACE

You are my hiding place. You will keep me out of trouble
and envelop me with songs that remind me I am free.
PSALM 32:7 VOICE

When the heat is on and you are feeling overwhelmed by life, don't forget that God is your hiding place. You can run into His arms at any time and be engulfed by His love. He will bless you with His protection, keeping you safe from the storms of life. They may come, but they will not pull you under. God will make sure of that. And He promises to whisper truths into your heart that remind you of the freedom Jesus bought with His life. There is no trouble too big for the Lord to prevail. There is no fear inside you He can't overcome. There are no bad decisions He can't realign with His will. And every time you run to God, you can rest assured He'll meet you right where you are and bring you into His goodness.

. . . .

Dear God, thank You for being a safe and secure
place for me! In the name of Jesus I pray. Amen.

19

HARD SEASONS
PRODUCE BLESSINGS

For you know that when your faith is tested it stirs up in you the power of endurance. And then as your endurance grows even stronger, it will release perfection into every part of your being until there is nothing missing and nothing lacking.

JAMES 1:3–4 TPT

In God's economy, He has a beautiful way of using hard seasons to produce fruit and blessing. There is no place or person on planet Earth that can replicate His magnificent work in the life of a believer. That's exactly why we need God to get us through the ups and downs of life. With Him, there is a domino effect of sorts, but it all starts with hardship. So be careful not to see tough times solely as a negative or as a punishment. It's through these circumstances we are blessed with endurance, and we'll eventually find ourselves full of His goodness and lacking in nothing.

* *

Dear God, thank You for bringing beauty from the ashes. In the name of Jesus I pray. Amen.

THE BLESSING OF BEING TIGHTLY WRAPPED

Tormented and empty are wicked and destructive people,
but the one who trusts in the Eternal is wrapped tightly
in His gracious love. Express your joy; be happy in Him,
you who are good and true. Go ahead, shout and rejoice
aloud, you whose hearts are honest and straightforward.

PSALM 32:10–11 VOICE

When you are wrapped tightly in God's love, you are freed to express the joy it brings. It allows you to be happy in your relationship with Him. You will find peace in the middle of your mess because of His graciousness. When you are committed in faith, it's worthy of a mighty shout to the heavens because He blesses that decision. And it's important to recognize we don't have to work to feel confident about following God. That blessing simply flows out of our hearts as we stand committed. So be honest and straightforward with the Lord because good things follow.

• •

Dear God, help me trust You so I feel held by
Your love. In the name of Jesus I pray. Amen.

21

ASKING FOR IT

And if anyone longs to be wise, ask God for wisdom
and he will give it! He won't see your lack of wisdom
as an opportunity to scold you over your failures but
he will overwhelm your failures with his generous
grace. Just make sure you ask empowered by confident
faith without doubting that you will receive.

JAMES 1:5–6 TPT

You're invited to be bold in asking because God understands the limitations of humanity. He knows where we will fall short and where our best won't be enough. Perfection was never His goal, which is a beautiful blessing in and of itself. It's a daily reminder that we need Him. So whatever it is you need, ask God for it. Do you need help forgiving? Ask. Need peace or joy? Ask. Need endurance? Ask. And friend, let wisdom be a daily and persistent request. Thanks to His generosity and kindness, rest assured you will be blessed with it.

. . . .

Dear God, I'm grateful I can ask in my lack and You will
bless in abundance. In the name of Jesus I pray. Amen.

MADE NEW BY JESUS

*He came to save us. It's not that we earned it by doing good
works or righteous deeds; He came because He is merciful.
He brought us out of our old ways of living to a new beginning
through the washing of regeneration; and He made us
completely new through the Holy Spirit, who was poured
out in abundance through Jesus the Anointed, our Savior.*

TITUS 3:5–6 VOICE

You've been made new. Through Jesus, you have been
regenerated, made spotless in the eyes of God. All those terrible
seasons of sinning are no longer hanging over your head. The
bad choices you made have been removed from the ledger.
The times you partnered with the world's wretchedness are
gone, washed from your record. What a blessing indeed! Keep
in mind this is because of His mercy. There's nothing you did to
clean yourself up. You aren't responsible for the transformation;
Jesus is. But friend, you are the beneficiary!

• •

*Dear God, thank You it wasn't up to me or my effort
to be made new. In the name of Jesus I pray. Amen.*

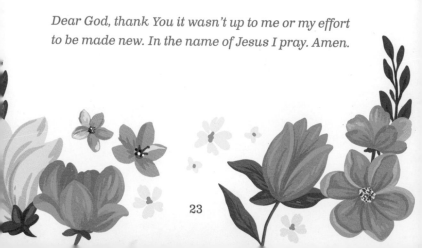

OUR CONSISTENT GOD

Every good gift bestowed, every perfect gift received
comes to us from above, courtesy of the Father of lights.
He is consistent. He won't change His mind or play tricks
in the shadows. We have a special role in His plan. He
calls us to life by His message of truth so that we will
show the rest of His creatures His goodness and love.
JAMES 1:17–18 VOICE

In a world where things are constantly changing, what a blessing to know God never does. His consistency is a stabilizing truth that helps steady our spirits. The God you read of in the Bible—the One who promised us beautiful things—is the same One you pray to today. He doesn't change His mind. He doesn't reverse course. There is nothing we can say to sway His plans or taint His thoughts. That means He is fully faithful and totally trustworthy. So be blessed knowing the God you serve is the same yesterday, today, and tomorrow. And He's perfect.

. . . .

Dear God, I'm blessed by the fact that You will
never change. In the name of Jesus I pray. Amen.

24

DRAWING A LINE IN THE SAND

If a person is causing divisions in the community,
warn him once; and if necessary, warn him twice.
After that, avoid him completely because by then you
are sure that you are dealing with a corrupt, sinful
person. He is determined to condemn himself.

TITUS 3:10–11 VOICE

You have God's authorization to confront the people who
are being divisive. You have His permission to set healthy
boundaries wherever necessary. And you also have the Lord's
blessing to walk away. Sometimes we think as Christian women
we should be agreeable above all else. We think we should
always bend over backward to accommodate others at our
expense. And while God asks us to live at peace whenever
possible, His intention is never for us to be a doormat. Let
today's scripture be a blessing as you realize you're free to
draw a line in the sand.

Dear God, help me realize I have Your permission
to set boundaries instead of being a doormat.
In the name of Jesus I pray. Amen.

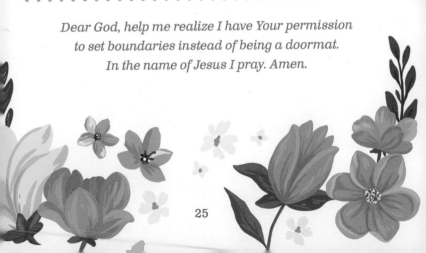

WATCHING YOUR WORDS

If you put yourself on a pedestal, thinking you have become a role model in all things religious, but you can't control your mouth, then think again. Your mouth exposes your heart, and your religion is useless.

JAMES 1:26 VOICE

What a very powerful reminder that our words matter. We can bless with them, encouraging others at the right time and in the right way. Or we can use them as weapons. They can get us into trouble in a split second, amen? So it's important we are kind and humble as we speak, being intentional to control what comes out of our mouths. The last thing we want to do is sound lofty, like we're holier, smarter, or better than others. And it's vital we remember that what is in our hearts spills out in our words. Ask God to purify you so nothing hinders your ability to be a blessing to those around you.

* *

Dear God, keep me humble in spirit and mindful of the words I use. In the name of Jesus I pray. Amen.

26

PUTTING OUR HOPE IN GOD

Don't put your life in the hands of experts who know
nothing of life, of salvation life. Mere humans don't
have what it takes; when they die, their projects die
with them. Instead, get help from the God of Jacob,
put your hope in GOD and know real blessing!
PSALM 146:3–5 MSG

One of the smartest decisions we can make is to anchor our hope in God and not in anything this world offers. So often, we listen to the "experts." We give them permission to choose and plot our course. But the truth is as humans we have limited knowledge. We can't see the big picture because we don't have all the details. And honestly, the world changes its mind all the time. Looking to the Lord for help sets us up for a beautiful blessing. You may have smart family and friends who have lots of life experiences and the best intentions, but nobody trumps the kind of love and support we have access to in God.

. . . .

Dear God, You are my answer to everything.
In the name of Jesus I pray. Amen.

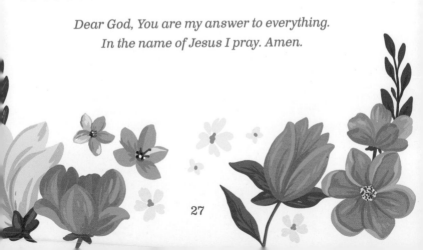

27

THE REMINDER

You keep all your promises. You are the Creator of heaven's glory, earth's grandeur, and the ocean's greatness. The oppressed get justice with you. The hungry are satisfied with you. Prisoners find their freedom with you. You open the eyes of the blind, and you fully restore those bent over with shame. You love those who love and honor you.

PSALM 146:6–8 TPT

This scripture makes a bold claim about God, and it's all true. He's a promise keeper. He's the Creator. He exacts justice and satisfies the hungry. He's the freedom giver and eye opener. God will always restore a sense of value to those crushed under the weight of shame. And oh yes, the Lord is the Lover of our souls. Sometimes we need a robust reminder of His majesty. We need to remember who He is and what He has done. Our weary hearts need a boost of truth to lighten the load we're carrying. And when we find that refreshment, we're deeply blessed by it.

. . . .

Dear God, when I forget Your magnificence and sovereignty, remind me. In the name of Jesus I pray. Amen.

28

BLESSING FOR OBEDIENCE

*If you listen closely to the voice of the Eternal your God
and carefully obey all the commands I'm giving you today,
He'll lift you up high above every other nation on earth.
All of the following blessings will be yours—in fact, they'll
chase after you—if you'll listen to what He tells you.*
DEUTERONOMY 28:1–2 VOICE

After speaking the words we read in today's scripture, Moses then went on to share the blessings that would follow the people's obedience, and it hit their hearts and homes. It affected the harvest, their children, their livestock. All things near and dear to them would prosper in abundance for following God's ways. It may look different today, but we will also experience blessings for obedience. When we focus on doing what He's asked of us, we'll reap a reward. Our yes to God's leading unlocks gifts from above. Of course a blessing isn't the only reason for our obedience, but it's a beautiful gift of recognition. Friend, where is God asking for your compliance today?

* *

Dear God, yes, I will obey. In the name of Jesus I pray. Amen.

WHAT WILL YOU CHOOSE?

So then, surrender to God. Stand up to the devil and
resist him and he will flee in agony. Move your heart
closer and closer to God, and he will come even closer
to you. But make sure you cleanse your life, you sinners,
and keep your heart pure and stop doubting.

JAMES 4:7–8 TPT

Every day we have a choice to make. With all the trials and temptations that come our way, will we give in to the devil or turn to God? Either we'll allow the enemy to scare us and stir us up or we'll run to the Lord for His blessing of peace. And while that answer seems like a no-brainer when the waters are still, it's smart to decide before they become tumultuous again. That way, the game plan is set and you know what to do. Every time you move closer to God, He will come even closer to you.

• •

Dear God, help me decide now to always
choose You! In the name of Jesus I pray. Amen.

WHEN GOD SAYS, "GO"

GOD told Abram: "Leave your country, your family, and your father's home for a land that I will show you. I'll make you a great nation and bless you. I'll make you famous; you'll be a blessing. I'll bless those who bless you; those who curse you I'll curse. All the families of the Earth will be blessed through you."
GENESIS 12:1–3 MSG

Sometimes we hear God tell us to go. It may be a gut feeling to step out of our comfort zone and try something new. It may be conviction to make changes in a relationship. We may feel called to take a stand or bend a knee. It might be a literal move across the country or a shift in perspective. Regardless, the result is always a blessing. When we are obedient and follow God in the easy and in the hard, He honors our commitment. He recognizes our faith. And a blessing follows.

• •

Dear God, help me follow Your lead and be blessed. In the name of Jesus I pray. Amen.

31

FLIRTING WITH THE WORLD

*You have become spiritual adulterers who are having
an affair, an unholy relationship with the world.
Don't you know that flirting with the world's values
places you at odds with God? Whoever chooses to
be the world's friend makes himself God's enemy!*

JAMES 4:4 TPT

What a strict warning about our tendency to love the world over the Lord, even going so far as to describe it as an adulterous relationship. It may seem a harsh comparison, but it's a powerful caution that can't help but catch our attention. Take inventory of your life over the past week. Would an outsider see you as someone in love with the world's ways? Or would they recognize that your allegiances lie with God instead? Your blessing will come when you embrace God over everything else, refusing to flirt with the world's values.

• •

*Dear God, my heart is Yours. Give me strength to
walk that out every day so I keep my eyes focused
on You. In the name of Jesus I pray. Amen.*

A CHILD OF GOD

He entered our world, a world He made; yet the world did not recognize Him. Even though He came to His own people, they refused to listen and receive Him. But for all who did receive and trust in Him, He gave them the right to be reborn as children of God; He bestowed this birthright not by human power or initiative but by God's will.

JOHN 1:10–13 VOICE

You are blessed to be called a child of God when you choose Him back. The Lord has moved in your heart, inviting you into the adventure of faith, and your yes in response seals you as His. Jesus stepped off the throne and into the world to change the trajectory of mankind. He blessed us through His sacrifice on the cross. And when we connect our hearts to His, recognizing Jesus as our Savior, we are reborn into the family of Christ. It becomes our birthright through His will.

. . . .

Dear God, I'm blessed that my birthright into Your family has been secured. In the name of Jesus I pray. Amen.

33

BLESSINGS FOR HUMILITY

Does the Scripture mean nothing to you that says, "The Spirit that God breathed into our hearts is a jealous Lover who intensely desires to have more and more of us"? But he continues to pour out more and more grace upon us. For it says, "God resists you when you are proud but continually pours out grace when you are humble."

JAMES 4:5–6 TPT

God promises to pour out His grace on those who are humble. Being humble means we recognize our position in relation to God's. We understand that His ways are better than our ways and that His thoughts are higher than our thoughts. When we're modest, giving credit to God, it lets Him know we believe all good things come from Him alone. And in our gratitude, being humble means we recognize that our abilities exist because He blessed us with them. God is ready to extend His grace and kindness to those who resist prideful attitudes.

. . . .

Dear God, help me remember the value of being humble. Everything good comes directly from You, and I know it. In the name of Jesus I pray. Amen.

FULLY SATISFY

*I am convinced that my God will fully satisfy every
need you have, for I have seen the abundant riches
of glory revealed to me through Jesus Christ!*

PHILIPPIANS 4:19 TPT

What a blessing to realize God is not only fully aware of every
need we have; He promises to fully satisfy each of them. Here's
where we get into trouble, though. So often when we ask God
to help us, we have a very specific idea in mind. We know what
we want and when we want it. But it takes mature faith to
understand that He has a perfect plan in mind and it doesn't
always align with ours. The truth is you can trust God. He knows
exactly what needs to happen to satisfy the lack in your life.
Rather than battle, let Him bless you.

. . . .

*Dear God, grow my faith so I trust You without question as You
work in my circumstances. You're God and I am not, and what
a beautiful blessing that is! In the name of Jesus I pray. Amen.*

UNENDING CONVERSATION, UNMATCHED PEACE

Don't be pulled in different directions or worried about a thing. Be saturated in prayer throughout each day, offering your faith-filled requests before God with overflowing gratitude. Tell him every detail of your life, then God's wonderful peace that transcends human understanding, will guard your heart and mind through Jesus Christ.

PHILIPPIANS 4:6–7 TPT

It's an honor to talk to God throughout the day. What a gift to know we can saturate our lives in prayer, telling Him what's heavy on our minds and hearts. How loved we are to have a God who has such compassion for those who love Him. And even more than that, what a blessing to know He will bring unmatched peace to our weary souls, keeping our thoughts guarded from the negative narrative designed to discourage and cause fear.

. . . .

Dear God, thank You that I can talk to You anytime and anywhere about anything. And thank You for the blessing of Your peace that is beyond our understanding. In the name of Jesus I pray. Amen.

BUT BECAUSE OF HIM

Blessed be God, the Father of our Lord Jesus the Anointed One, who grants us every spiritual blessing in these heavenly realms where we live in the Anointed—not because of anything we have done, but because of what He has done for us.

EPHESIANS 1:3 VOICE

Scripture tells us that God has granted every spiritual blessing in the heavenly realms to those who love Him. These blessings include being chosen, being adopted as His, being accepted through Jesus, and being redeemed. And what a relief to know that none of His generosity is dependent on what we do or how we act. There is nothing we can muster in our own strength to ignite His kindness. God's love is constant and unchanging, something incomparable anywhere in the world.

. . . .

Dear God, I bless You for being sovereign. I'm so grateful for Your love and compassion; let me never take it for granted. It's all about You and because of You, and I recognize that. Thank You for being unmatched and incomparable. I love You with all my heart! In the name of Jesus I pray. Amen.

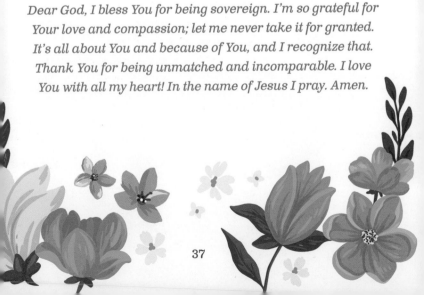

WHERE TO FIX YOUR THOUGHTS

Keep your thoughts continually fixed on all that is authentic and real, honorable and admirable, beautiful and respectful, pure and holy, merciful and kind. And fasten your thoughts on every glorious work of God, praising him always. Put into practice the example of all that you have heard from me or seen in my life and the God of peace will be with you in all things.

PHILIPPIANS 4:8–9 TPT

It's important we keep our thoughts in check because it's easy to let our minds drift to everything that is wrong, filling our hearts with worry and fear. It's easy to look down the path to see horrible outcomes and endings. But nothing about that is life-giving. Instead, it robs us of peace. It makes us doubt God's sovereignty. And it makes us hopeless. There is a blessing that comes with keeping our thoughts fixed on what is authentic, beautiful, honorable, and holy. That blessing is His perfect presence being with us always.

. . . .

Dear God, help me stay focused on You rather than any scary circumstance that surrounds me. In the name of Jesus I pray. Amen.

HEARING AND BELIEVING

Because you, too, have heard the word of truth—the good
news of your salvation—and because you believed in the
One who is truth, your lives are marked with His seal.
This is none other than the Holy Spirit who was promised.
EPHESIANS 1:13 VOICE

There is a weighty connection between hearing and believing.
Too often, people hear the truth about God and learn about His
story through the Word, but it stops there. They understand
He is all-powerful. They recognize there are blessings that
come from a relationship with Him. But they never move from
the hearing phase into believing faith. God has chosen you
and provided every opportunity for you to embrace the good
news of your salvation. When you hear, believe, and choose
Him back, He blesses you through the gift of the Holy Spirit.
And you are forever His.

• •

Dear God, thank You for choosing me to hear the Word
of truth and the good news of salvation. My heart is
full knowing I am Yours forever. Bless my life as I
bless others. In the name of Jesus I pray. Amen.

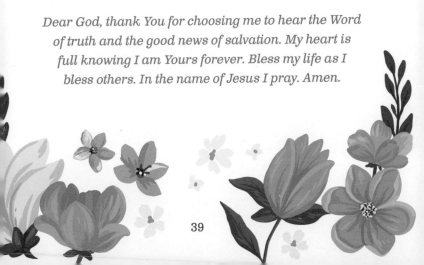

HOW DO YOU WANT TO BE TREATED?

"Don't pick on people, jump on their failures, criticize their faults—unless, of course, you want the same treatment. Don't condemn those who are down; that hardness can boomerang. Be easy on people; you'll find life a lot easier."

LUKE 6:37 MSG

The Golden Rule tells us to treat others the way we want to be treated. If we want to be treated with kindness, then we should be kind. If we want to be forgiven when we offend others, then we should be quick to extend grace when offended. If we want to be met with compassion, then we need to be compassionate in the ways we relate to those around us. Life is hard enough without having a hard heart toward one another. Let's be women who make this world a better place. And when we do, it sets us up to be blessed back.

. . . .

Dear God, show me when to stand up and when to stand down. Remind me to treat others the way I want to be treated. In the name of Jesus I pray. Amen.

40

THE BLESSING OF SELFLESS LIVING

"Give away your life; you'll find life given back, but not merely given back—given back with bonus and blessing. Giving, not getting, is the way. Generosity begets generosity."
LUKE 6:38 MSG

There is a blessing that comes from being selfless. When we are more focused on giving than getting, good things naturally flow from that mindset. When we are kind and generous with our resources, we will find the same when we are in need. In God's economy, there is always a blessing that comes from having a servant's attitude. As you look at your life, where do you need to change things? Where can you focus on the needs of others above your own? If this is a struggle for you, ask God to align your heart with His. He will honor your request and bless you for it.

. . . .

Dear God, I confess the times I have put my needs above others'. Help me develop selflessness so I can impact the lives of those around me. In the name of Jesus I pray. Amen.

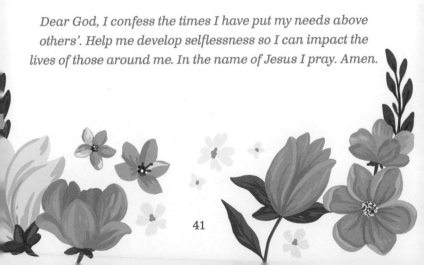

EXPERIENCING
WHOLEHEARTEDNESS

*But now that you've found you don't have to listen to sin
tell you what to do, and have discovered the delight of
listening to God telling you, what a surprise! A whole,
healed, put-together life right now, with more and
more of life on the way! Work hard for sin your whole
life and your pension is death. But God's gift is real
life, eternal life, delivered by Jesus, our Master.*
ROMANS 6:22–23 MSG

Scripture says we can experience wholeheartedness when
we focus on God. When we are intentional to shut our ears
to the world's offerings and promises, it frees us to hear His
voice instead. And it's vital we grab on to this promise because
we will never thrive when we work for our sin instead of our
God. Ask the Lord to reveal any hidden sin so He can heal you
from it. And share your gratitude for the blessing of salvation
that Jesus made possible.

. . . .

*Dear God, give me the confidence to reject
sin and embrace Your perfect plan for my
life. In the name of Jesus I pray. Amen.*

BE EXTRAORDINARY

If you want to be extraordinary—love your enemies! Do good without restraint! Lend with abandon! Don't expect anything in return! Then you'll receive the truly great reward—you will be children of the Most High—for God is kind to the ungrateful and those who are wicked. So imitate God and be truly compassionate, the way your Father is.

LUKE 6:35–36 VOICE

While we may want to be extraordinary, once we see what it requires, it can leave us discouraged. It's easy to love the lovable, but we're to love our enemies? We're to lavish our good works on others? To be extraordinary, we should lend freely and expect nothing back? Reading this almost makes us give up the fight to be something special—to be called children of God. But understand that once we're filled with faith and trusting God to help us walk according to His will, He will bless us with what we need to have this kind of compassion.

. . . .

Dear God, help me imitate Your compassion to the world around me. In the name of Jesus I pray. Amen.

43

THE DAILY BATTLE

"A thief has only one thing in mind—he wants to steal, slaughter, and destroy. But I have come to give you everything in abundance, more than you expect—life in its fullness until you overflow!"
JOHN 10:10 TPT

What a stark contrast between what the enemy wants for us and what God has planned. There is a daily battle for our peace and joy that forces us to choose sides. And the deciding factor is faith. The question becomes whether you will stand firm in faith or entertain the enemy's chaos. There are a million things every day that are designed to take us out. There is every kind of terrible to stir us up. But keeping our minds steadfast on God brings us life to the fullest. It blesses us with His abundance!

. . . .

Dear God, I recognize the daily choice I have to rest in You or live stressed. Help me cling to You so I can experience the overflow of Your goodness. In the name of Jesus I pray. Amen.

44

USING WORDS TO BLESS

It's the same with people. A person full of goodness
in his heart produces good things; a person with
an evil reservoir in his heart pours out evil things.
The heart overflows in the words a person speaks;
your words reveal what's within your heart.

LUKE 6:45 VOICE

I want my words to bless You, revealing the commitment I have to follow Your will and ways with gusto. Let them be a beautiful overflow of our time spent together. And let my speech be the giveaway of the goodness stored in my heart for others. From the blessings I receive through You, I want my life to be a blessing to those around me. I am Yours, Lord. Mature me and use me for Your purposes.

. . . .

Dear God, let the words that overflow from my heart
glorify You. I want to be so filled with what matters most
to You that I bring Your goodness into the lives of others
with what I say. Bless me with powerful words of truth
and compassion. In the name of Jesus I pray. Amen.

GOD KNOWS WHAT HE IS DOING

*"I know what I'm doing. I have it all planned
out—plans to take care of you, not abandon
you, plans to give you the future you hope for."*
JEREMIAH 29:11 MSG

What a blessing to know that God is in complete control. How wonderful to understand that He is fully aware of what He's doing, following the plan He set in motion before the creation of the world. Take a deep breath, friend. God is involved in the details of our lives. He's a planner, which means He knows what needs to happen to take care of those who love Him. The Lord knows when to intervene and when to let us walk things out in faith. And He knows when we need some encouragement that things will be okay and when we need Him to deposit a heaping dose of hope into our hearts.

• •

*Dear God, what a relief to know You have everything
planned out. What a blessing to know I'm not on my
own in this life. In the name of Jesus I pray. Amen.*

46

IN THE SAME MEASURE

If you don't want to be judged, don't judge. If you don't want to be condemned, don't condemn. If you want to be forgiven, forgive. Don't hold back—give freely, and you'll have plenty poured back into your lap—a good measure, pressed down, shaken together, brimming over. You'll receive in the same measure you give.

LUKE 6:37–38 VOICE

Some may read today's scripture and feel encouraged. But some may read it and feel hopeless. This is a powerful concept unpacked. The truth that says we receive in the measure we give has the potential to be a big, beautiful blessing from God Himself. So be challenged to live in ways that bring blessings on you all while blessing those around you too. Live how you want to be treated, and love the way you want to be loved.

• •

Dear God, remind me to be thoughtful in how I treat others because it matters. Make me aware of how I love those around me so I'm set up to receive a blessing back. In the name of Jesus I pray. Amen.

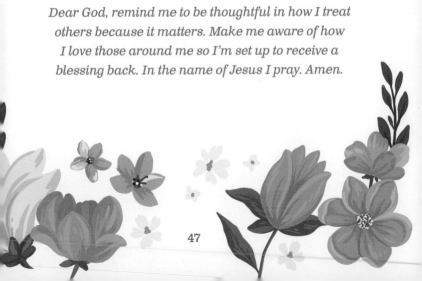

47

TURNING THINGS AROUND

"Yes, when you get serious about finding me and want it more than anything else, I'll make sure you won't be disappointed." GOD's Decree. "I'll turn things around for you. I'll bring you back from all the countries into which I drove you"—GOD's Decree—"bring you home to the place from which I sent you off into exile. You can count on it."

JEREMIAH 29:13–14 MSG

We can experience the blessing of restoration when we trust God. Rather than try to fix things ourselves or look to worldly solutions, when we're honest and seek His help above all else, He will turn things around. Where do you need God right now? Are you struggling in an important relationship? Are you scared about upcoming changes? Are you unsettled about the future? Do you feel hopeless? Go to God and let Him bless you and comfort you as He restores those empty and broken places.

. . . .

Dear God, please intervene in my situation and do what only You can do. Turn things around so I can find joy and peace again. In the name of Jesus I pray. Amen.

48

SET YOUR GAZE ON LIBERTY

*But those who set their gaze deeply into the perfecting
law of liberty are fascinated by and respond to the
truth they hear and are strengthened by it—they
experience God's blessing in all that they do!*

JAMES 1:25 TPT

Jesus came to set us free. That means we no longer have to be in bondage to our sin. The problem is that many of us don't grab on to this blessing of liberty. Maybe we don't think we deserve it. Maybe we don't think it's for real. Maybe we are scared to harness its power in our lives, afraid to be let down one more time. But be careful not to discredit Jesus' gift because it's a game changer. Scripture says if we set our gaze on it, we will be strengthened. And we will experience God's blessing on the regular.

• •

*Dear God, help me lock my eyes on the beautiful blessing
of Jesus. Strengthen me as I stand on the promise of
freedom in You. In the name of Jesus I pray. Amen.*

49

THE GIFT OF THE HOLY SPIRIT

So answer me this: Did the Holy Spirit come to you as a reward for keeping Jewish laws? No, you received him as a gift because you believed in the Messiah. Your new life began when the Holy Spirit gave you a new birth. Why then would you so foolishly turn from living in the Spirit by trying to finish by your own works?
GALATIANS 3:2–3 TPT

God's Spirit in us—it's a huge blessing to know there's nothing we can do to make it happen. In the same vein, there is nothing we can do to mess it up either. The gift of the Holy Spirit is the beautiful reward we receive for trusting Jesus to be our personal Savior. God chose us to be His and we responded with a resounding yes! That heartfelt decision was all it took to ensure God's presence would be with us always. Now that's a blessing indeed.

* *

Dear God, I'm so grateful for the gift of Your Holy Spirit. Help me trust You rather than rely on my own resources. In the name of Jesus I pray. Amen.

THE LAW VERSUS HIS GRACE

Through this man we all receive gifts of grace beyond our imagination. You see, Moses gave us rules to live by, but Jesus the Anointed offered us gifts of grace and truth. God, unseen until now, is revealed in the Voice, God's only Son, straight from the Father's heart.

JOHN 1:16–18 VOICE

Jesus was a game changer. Until then, people lived by the law of Moses. Of course, it was inspired by God, but the rules Moses laid down were strictly enforced and strictly followed. When the Messiah came to earth, the rules transformed into gifts of grace and truth. The rigidity of living was removed. And today we're blessed to live in freedom. Ask God to help you grab on to grace and truth so you don't fall back into rules and regulations. Embrace all that Jesus did for you!

• •

Dear God, I confess my tendency to live by the law, even if I'm the one who establishes it. Help me instead to thrive in the grace and truth of Jesus Christ. In the name of Jesus I pray. Amen.

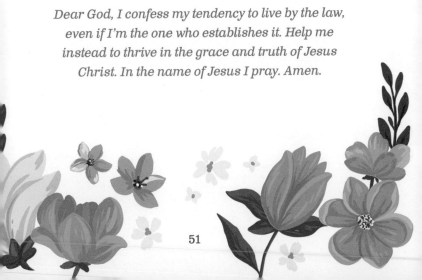

51

AND GENTILES TOO

And the Scripture prophesied that on the basis of faith God would declare gentiles to be righteous. God announced the good news ahead of time to Abraham: "Through your example of faith, all the nations will be blessed!" And so the blessing of Abraham's faith is now our blessing too!

GALATIANS 3:8–9 TPT

God declared that Gentiles could be right with Him through faith. Not only did He make a way for Jews to be in a relationship with Him, but the Lord made a way for everyone else to as well. No one was left out! God's goodness extends to everyone who receives the gift of salvation through His Son. It's a blessing to realize He thought of you before the creation of the world and chose you to be His. Hallelujah!

. . . .

Dear God, my heart is full of gratitude as I realize Your heart's desire to leave no one behind. You unlocked eternity for everyone who puts their faith in You. I'm thankful for being blessed forever. In the name of Jesus I pray. Amen.

NO MATTER WHAT

Be cheerful no matter what; pray all the time; thank
God no matter what happens. This is the way God
wants you who belong to Christ Jesus to live.
1 THESSALONIANS 5:16–18 MSG

Talk about a challenge! It's not easy to thank God when your life has blown up. It can feel impossible to be cheerful when you're in the middle of a divorce or a bankruptcy or the loss of someone close to you. And making prayer a priority when you're barely keeping your head above water feels like a setup for failure. But friend, if this is the way God is asking us to live, then we can rest assured He will give us the ability to do it. He will bless us with strength to walk it out. Because it requires faith, be quick to ask Him to help make it so.

. . . .

Dear God, I need Your help to have the kind of no-
matter-what faith You're asking of me. Fill me with
grace and ability. In the name of Jesus I pray. Amen.

53

CEASE STRIVING

*God provides for His own. It is pointless to get up
early, work hard, and go to bed late anxiously
laboring for food to eat; for God provides for
those He loves, even while they are sleeping.*

PSALM 127:2 VOICE

Simply stated, stop striving and trust God. Today's verse
is powerful because it shifts our perspective to the truth.
Sometimes we get stuck on the treadmill of life, trying to work
our way to goodness. We focus on doing rather than trusting.
We spend our time strategizing, looking for creative ways to
make ends meet. And instead of finding long-term success, we
end up exhausted. Believing God will always provide for you
requires a leap of faith, especially when your situation feels
hopeless, but that doesn't negate truth. Friend, cease striving
and give God the space to bless you.

. . . .

*Dear God, I confess that I do trust in my own ways
and my own understanding when I should be relying
on You. Help me give up control and wait for Your
blessing. In the name of Jesus I pray. Amen.*

54

HOLY AND WHOLE

*May God himself, the God who makes everything holy
and whole, make you holy and whole, put you together—
spirit, soul, and body—and keep you fit for the coming
of our Master, Jesus Christ. The One who called you
is completely dependable. If he said it, he'll do it!*

1 THESSALONIANS 5:23–24 MSG

Many of us feel broken by life. Maybe it was the loss of a child
or the loss of a parent. Maybe we experienced a trauma that has
left us shaken. Maybe we feel abandoned, unlovable. Maybe we
feel broken because of a moral failure on our part that affected
important relationships negatively. Maybe we're descending
into despair a little more each day. If that's you, be encouraged
by knowing God can make everything and everyone holy and
whole. He can put you back together. Because He's faithful to
His Word, believe God will do it.

. . . .

*Dear God, please restore me and my broken heart. Bless
me as You piece me back together and make me holy
and whole again. In the name of Jesus I pray. Amen.*

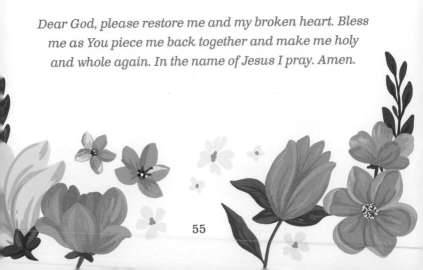

55

HIS HAND IS ON YOU

So be content with who you are, and don't put on airs. God's strong hand is on you; he'll promote you at the right time. Live carefree before God; he is most careful with you.
1 PETER 5:6–7 MSG

God always knows the perfect time to promote those who put their faith in Him. He understands the skills and experiences that need collecting first. The Lord knows the perfect sequence of events that need to precede and follow. It's important you understand the blessing of His timing. When you choose to follow God's lead, your heart will be at peace. You won't have to act strong. You won't have to act brave. You can rest knowing that the Lord's hand is on you and that He will always hold you with care and compassion.

· ·

Dear God, mature my faith so I can surrender my expectations and trust Your plans instead. Let me believe in Your blessing over my blueprint. I know Your mighty hand is on my life. In the name of Jesus I pray. Amen.

OVERWHELMED

Yes, God is more than ready to overwhelm you with every form of grace, so that you will have more than enough of everything—every moment and in every way. He will make you overflow with abundance in every good thing you do.

2 CORINTHIANS 9:8 TPT

In a world where we find ourselves overwhelmed all the time— swamped by schedules, situations, and sadness—what a blessing to know God is ready to overwhelm us with every form of His grace. That isn't a promise that the busyness will go away, but it is a promise that we will have what we need every moment and in every way. We will live in abundance. So when you are feeling exhausted by life, let God bless you with His overflow. Let Him help you face each challenge with grace.

. . . .

Dear God, thank You for this reminder of Your promise to be in the details of my life. Thank You for the blessing of abundance, promising You will give me more than enough as I navigate the ups and downs of life. In the name of Jesus I pray. Amen.

SUFFERING IS FOR A SEASON

So keep a firm grip on the faith. The suffering won't last forever. It won't be long before this generous God who has great plans for us in Christ—eternal and glorious plans they are!—will have you put together and on your feet for good. He gets the last word; yes, he does.

1 PETER 5:9–11 MSG

Be blessed in knowing that suffering won't last forever. We'll no doubt face times of tremendous hardship in every way—physically, emotionally, relationally, financially—but it will be short-lived. Every one of us will experience both the dark valleys and the mountaintops. We'll each have to navigate grief and sadness and heartache. But at the right time according to God's will, we will find relief. We'll be blessed with healing and restoration. And God will enable us to get back on our feet and press on.

. . . .

Dear God, it's encouraging to know suffering won't last forever. Thank You for the blessing of limits. I know Your timing is perfect and Your plan powerful. In the name of Jesus I pray. Amen.

PLUS MORE

This generous God who supplies abundant seed for the
farmer, which becomes bread for our meals, is even
more extravagant toward you. First he supplies every
need, plus more. Then he multiplies the seed as you sow
it, so that the harvest of your generosity will grow.
2 CORINTHIANS 9:10 TPT

Just like every good parent, God makes provision for our needs.
If it matters to you, it matters to Him. He understands you
need financial means to make ends meet. He knows you need a
strong community of support. God understands you need love
and acceptance and to feel significant. The Lord knows every
basic need and every complex need. And it's because of His
great generosity that He chooses to meet them—plus more. The
blessing comes not only in His provision but in His abundance.

• •

Dear God, I'm always blown away by Your kindness
and generosity toward me. You not only provide, but
You go above that to bless. I praise Your name and give
You the glory! In the name of Jesus I pray. Amen.

HELP IN EVERY SITUATION

*"Do not yield to fear, for I am always near. Never turn
your gaze from me, for I am your faithful God. I will infuse
you with my strength and help you in every situation.
I will hold you firmly with my victorious right hand."*

ISAIAH 41:10 TPT

When God says He will help you in every situation, it's not just
lip service. When He promises to infuse you with His own
strength, it's not an empty promise. God tells you not to give
in to fear because He's close by. And the Lord vows to hold you
firmly and victoriously because He loves you and is deeply
invested in your life. No matter what you are facing, God is
there. Embrace that truth and be blessed.

. . . .

*Dear God, what a relief to know You're with me in
every situation and will provide the help I need to get
to the other side. Because of Your presence, I will not
be afraid. Instead I'll stand in victory, blessed by Your
goodness! In the name of Jesus I pray. Amen.*

EVERYTHING IS GOING TO WORK OUT

That clinches it—help's coming, an answer's on the way, everything's going to work out. See those people polishing their chariots, and those others grooming their horses? But we're making garlands for GOD our God. The chariots will rust, those horses pull up lame—and we'll be on our feet, standing tall.

PSALM 20:6–8 MSG

Sometimes what we need more than anything is a reminder that things are going to work out. We need to know that help is on the way. In the middle of our mess, we need reassurance that our prayers are heard and an answer is on the horizon. It's our faith that offers comfort as we wait for God to show up. The world has nothing for us, and every solution it offers is a dead end. So grab on to the blessing that guarantees God is always with you and for you.

Dear God, thank You for the promise of an answer. Thank You for the promise of a resolution. Bless me with the strength to trust in You in all things. In the name of Jesus I pray. Amen.

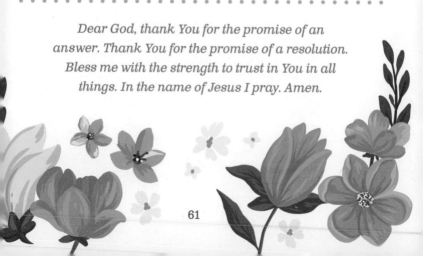

TRUTHS TO EMBRACE

The Eternal One bless and keep you. May He make His face shine upon you and be gracious to you. The Eternal lift up His countenance to look upon you and give you peace.
NUMBERS 6:24–26 VOICE

Let this passage of scripture wash over you in a new way today. It's such a beautiful and powerful promise that has the ability to tender the heart of every believer. God is so good, and He loves you so much. He is the one who blesses you. He is the one who keeps you. God is the one who is gracious to you. He is the one who gives you peace. Imagine how it would change things if you truly embraced these truths. Ask Him to make each of these weighty statements real in your everyday life.

· ·

Dear God, sometimes I don't feel worthy of Your love. In many ways, I feel more like a burden than a blessing. Let today's scripture sink deep in my DNA. In the name of Jesus I pray. Amen.

JESUS EMPTIED HIMSELF

He existed in the form of God, yet he gave no thought to seizing equality with God as his supreme prize. Instead he emptied himself of his outward glory by reducing himself to the form of a lowly servant. He became human!

PHILIPPIANS 2:6-7 TPT

Can you even imagine what it took for Jesus to empty Himself enough to be born, entering the world He created as a helpless infant? He chose to become human to save the world from sin and show us a better way. And the blessing is the opportunity to have a personal relationship with Him that leads to eternal life. Take some time today to reflect on this selfless act of Jesus. Think about how His life has changed yours. And give Him glory for changing the trajectory of mankind forever.

. . . .

Dear God, I'm so grateful You chose to step off Your throne and into my world to save me. That blesses me in every possible way. And my heart is full of thanksgiving for the sacrifices made for me. Thank You! In the name of Jesus I pray. Amen.

THE HOLY SPIRIT'S SUPPORT

Meanwhile, the moment we get tired in the waiting,
God's Spirit is right alongside helping us along. If
we don't know how or what to pray, it doesn't matter.
He does our praying in and for us, making prayer
out of our wordless sighs, our aching groans.
ROMANS 8:26 MSG

When we grow weary as we wait for God's answer to prayer, the Holy Spirit helps us. In those moments when we don't know how or what to pray, the Spirit interprets our groans and moans and prays on our behalf. He is our helper, and we're blessed to have such a wonderful advocate to support us in this life. The moment you said yes to a faith-filled life, God's Holy Spirit took up residence in you. That means the Lord's presence is with you always, prompting and guiding in every situation. What a gift!

. . . .

Dear God, thank You for the Holy Spirit and all the
ways I am blessed through Him. What a comfort
to know You are with me every day and in every
way. In the name of Jesus I pray. Amen.

REVITALIZED PASSION

*Now you must continue to make this new life fully
manifested as you live in the holy awe of God—
which brings you trembling into his presence. God
will continually revitalize you, implanting within
you the passion to do what pleases him.*

PHILIPPIANS 2:12–13 TPT

Sometimes we worry we'll lose our desire to do the work God has created and planned for us. We wonder if we'll become overwhelmed and burn out. We worry about compassion fatigue. And we think the work might become mundane and we will lose interest. But God has thought of everything! Scripture tells us He will revitalize us, reigniting passion to do the work He's set forth. Friend, you will be continually blessed with the strength and wisdom and motivation to walk out the calling He's placed on your life. Praise God!

. . . .

*Dear God, what a blessing to know You will
continually revitalize our passion for the work
You want us to do to further Your kingdom. I am
always amazed by Your unmatched awesomeness.
In the name of Jesus I pray. Amen.*

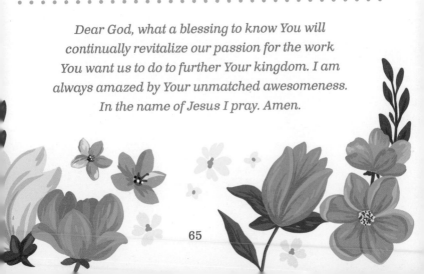

GOD'S COMFORTING LOVE

*Look at how much encouragement you've found in
your relationship with the Anointed One! You are
filled to overflowing with his comforting love. You have
experienced a deepening friendship with the Holy
Spirit and have felt his tender affection and mercy.*

PHILIPPIANS 2:1 TPT

There are seasons in life when we are desperate to be filled to overflowing with God's comforting love. Maybe you are about to become an empty nester. Maybe you advocated for yourself, and it wasn't well received by others. Maybe you're battling fear and loneliness. Maybe where you are right now is in the opposite direction of where you expected to be at this stage of life. Friend, don't discount the affection and mercy available to you through God's Holy Spirit. Let Him be your encouragement. Let Him be your friend. And be blessed knowing you are never expected to navigate life alone.

* * *

*Dear God, today I am asking to be filled to overflowing
with Your comforting love. Let Your presence through
the Holy Spirit bring encouragement to my weary
soul. In the name of Jesus I pray. Amen.*

WE CAN BE CONFIDENT

We are confident that God is able to orchestrate everything
to work toward something good and beautiful when we love
Him and accept His invitation to live according to His plan.
ROMANS 8:28 VOICE

Do you see the powerful cause and effect? Today's scripture reminds us that when we choose to not only love God but also embrace the plan He has for our lives, we can have unwavering confidence. We can know without a doubt that He has the unique ability to guarantee that everything will work together for our good in the end. It's a blessing to realize all the messiness will end up beautiful if we trust God. The tough seasons will be reconciled when we follow His plan. And we can be assured that the Lord's mighty hand is always at work for our benefit and His glory.

. . . .

Dear God, give me the strength and faith to trust You in
the darkest of days. I know that when my confidence is
secured in Your ability, You'll bring forth good things from
the difficulties I face. In the name of Jesus I pray. Amen.

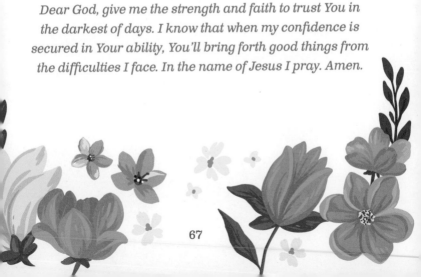

67

BE A NEON BILLBOARD

*I pray that you will continually experience
the immeasurable greatness of God's power
made available to you through faith. Then
your lives will be an advertisement of this
immense power as it works through you!*
EPHESIANS 1:19 TPT

What a blessing to know we can continually experience the
unmatched goodness of God in our lives. If we're looking
through the lens of faith, we'll be able to see His power at
work in our circumstances. And what's more, His mighty hand
in our lives will be a neon billboard to others. They'll find
encouragement and strength because of what they've seen
Him do through our situation. Only in God's economy can your
blessing turn around and bless those around you. Friend, ask
the Lord to open your eyes to see His immeasurable greatness.

. . . .

*Dear God, be a continuous force in my life. Help me
embrace Your greatness in everything I face. And let Your
power through my circumstances be a neon billboard
to show others the compassion and power You have for
those who love You. In the name of Jesus I pray. Amen.*

BORN AGAIN

So don't you see that we don't owe this old do-it-yourself life one red cent. There's nothing in it for us, nothing at all. The best thing to do is give it a decent burial and get on with your new life. God's Spirit beckons. There are things to do and places to go!

ROMANS 8:12–14 MSG

When you become a believer by acknowledging Jesus as the Son of God who died for your sins on the cross and rose again three days later, you are given a new life. You may have heard it called being *born again*. This rebirth is such a blessing because it erases every sin and washes us clean in the sight of God. Today's scripture is warning us to continue moving forward rather than turn back toward our old life—our old ways. We're a new creation in Christ, now empowered to live in ways that bless us and glorify God. Ask for His help, and it will be given!

• •

Dear God, I am ready for the adventure of a faith-filled life with You! In the name of Jesus I pray. Amen.

69

ADVENTUROUSLY EXPECTANT

This resurrection life you received from God is not a timid, grave-tending life. It's adventurously expectant, greeting God with a childlike "What's next, Papa?" God's Spirit touches our spirits and confirms who we really are. We know who he is, and we know who we are: Father and children.

ROMANS 8:15–16 MSG

Be adventurously expectant in your relationship with God. Have a childlike excitement for what's ahead as you follow Him with passion and purpose. The life of a believer is never meant to be boring. You're not to live in fear of what God has ordained in your life. He never intended for you to feel weak or insignificant or unloved. Instead, faith in the Lord should confirm your identity. It should open your eyes to His sovereignty. And it will bless you to embrace the truth that you're a child of the one and only God!

. . . .

Dear God, bless me with the ability to live adventurously expectant for what's next. Give me excitement to walk out my faith every day. In the name of Jesus I pray. Amen.

70

YOU'RE A MODEL

And here's what I want you to teach the older women:
Be respectful. Steer clear of gossip or drinking too much
so that you can teach what is good to young women.
Be a positive example, showing them what it is to love
their husbands and children, and teaching them to
control themselves in every way and to be pure.
TITUS 2:3–5 VOICE

Our lives preach. What we say and how we act is always being watched. But rather than become paranoid or stressed out, receive this truth as a blessing. God is trusting us to help mold and shape the next generation. He is calling us to train up godly women to be a blessing to their families and communities. In this arena, we're His hands and feet. And it's our privilege and burden to model faithful living to the younger women in our circle of influence.

. . . .

Dear God, give me the confidence to be a blessing
to the younger women in my community. Let my
words and actions encourage them to live and
love well. In the name of Jesus I pray. Amen.

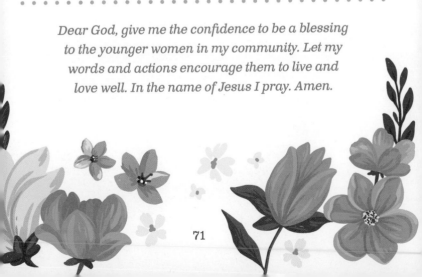

71

THE BLESSING OF CLARITY

*So let's keep focused on that goal, those of us who want
everything God has for us. If any of you have something
else in mind, something less than total commitment,
God will clear your blurred vision—you'll see it yet!
Now that we're on the right track, let's stay on it.*

PHILIPPIANS 3:15–16 MSG

With the busyness of our schedules, sometimes it's easy to lose
sight of what we're working toward. We get sidetracked by the
details of life and they drag us down. We see a shiny object,
and it catches our attention and leads us down the wrong path.
We forget what's important. But God says He will clear up our
blurred vision, refocusing our hearts and minds on what He
has set before us. The Lord will bless us with clarity.

. . . .

*Dear God, I confess that I can easily drift off course.
Life is busy and rigorous and often pulls me in a
different direction. Thank You for being the great
course corrector. In the name of Jesus I pray. Amen.*

72

LIVING GOD'S WAY

But what happens when we live God's way? He brings gifts into our lives, much the same way that fruit appears in an orchard—things like affection for others, exuberance about life, serenity. We develop a willingness to stick with things, a sense of compassion in the heart, and a conviction that a basic holiness permeates things and people.

GALATIANS 5:22 MSG

This verse should be the encouragement you need to make changes in your life that reflect your faith in God. There are many powerful scriptures that speak right to our hearts, and this is one of them. God sees our focus and effort to follow Him. When we choose to live for the Lord with passion and purpose—not perfection—He will bring blessings in abundance. Yes, friend, you will be blessed for intentionally pursuing godly living.

. . . .

Dear God, I want my life to be focused on living the way You intended. Give me courage to follow You no matter what. In the name of Jesus I pray. Amen.

73

YOU DON'T HAVE TO BE AN EXPERT

Friends, don't get me wrong: By no means do I count myself an expert in all of this, but I've got my eye on the goal, where God is beckoning us onward—to Jesus. I'm off and running, and I'm not turning back.
PHILIPPIANS 3:13–14 MSG

How refreshing to realize we don't have to have it all figured out. We don't have to be experts in the faith. We can make mistakes because we serve a God of second chances. And third chances. He will *always* extend grace as we try to walk out our faith. What's important is that we're focused on following God's will for our lives, that we're unwilling to walk away when things get hard. God is in this with us, and He will bless us in every way as we surrender to Him.

• •

Dear God, what a blessing to realize I don't have to do everything flawlessly. There is no expectation of perfection. You see my heart and my hope. Thank You! In the name of Jesus I pray. Amen.

SAVED AT OUR MESSIEST

*Now, would anyone dare to die for the sake of a
wicked person? We can all understand if someone
was willing to die for a truly noble person. But Christ
proved God's passionate love for us by dying in
our place while we were still lost and ungodly!*

ROMANS 5:7–8 TPT

What a compassionate God we serve! What a blessing to know
He came to save us when we were at our messiest. He sent His
Son to die for our sins when we were deep in our wretchedness.
It's easy to sacrifice for the grateful. We can love the lovable.
We can be selfless for the selfless. But God blessed us through
Jesus' death when we deserved death ourselves. Meditate on
that today.

• •

*Dear God, my heart is so tendered at the thought of You
sending Your Son into the world to die for my sins. I'm
so grateful for the blessing of Your unshakable love.
Let my life always be a reflection of my unshakable
thanksgiving! In the name of Jesus I pray. Amen.*

THE BLESSINGS
WHEN WE TRUST

*But those who trust in the Eternal One will regain
their strength. They will soar on wings as eagles.
They will run—never winded, never weary.
They will walk—never tired, never faint.*
ISAIAH 40:31 VOICE

If we stand in agreement with today's scripture, choosing to trust God when we're weak and weary, we will regain our strength. We'll be blessed to weather the storm. We'll be blessed with endurance for long-suffering. And we'll be blessed with God's peace—the kind that makes no sense to the world—regardless of whether we're in the dark valley or on the mountaintop. So often our tendency is to pull the covers over our heads and hide when things get tough. We ball up in a fetal position when it looks hopeless. Today, be encouraged to trust God in all situations and every circumstance.

* *

*Dear God, I love the simplicity of today's verse. But I also
know how difficult it can be to walk out. Grow my faith so
I can trust with ease! In the name of Jesus I pray. Amen.*

76

A THIRTY-THOUSAND-FOOT VIEW

But that's not all! Even in times of trouble we have a joyful confidence, knowing that our pressures will develop in us patient endurance. And patient endurance will refine our character, and proven character leads us back to hope.

ROMANS 5:3–4 TPT

When you're in the thick of it, all you can see are horrible outcomes. But when you take a thirty-thousand-foot view of the difficult circumstances you're facing—adding in your faith— you'll see what's going on with clarity. You will be able to see the fruit to come from the trouble. You will have joyful confidence in God's hand over your situation. And you'll find supernatural strength and endurance to stand strong through the refining process that will lead to hope. It's a blessing that God wastes nothing and supernaturally manages the details of our lives!

. . . .

Dear God, it's so amazing how our times of trouble can lead us back to hope. I don't always understand Your ways, but I deeply appreciate them. You are simply amazing! In the name of Jesus I pray. Amen.

THE ONE WHO NEVER CHANGES

The grass withers, the flower fades as the breath of the Eternal One blows away. People are no different from grass. The grass withers, the flower fades; nothing lasts except the word of our God. It will stand forever.
ISAIAH 40:7–8 VOICE

In a world where everything withers and fades, let's raise a hallelujah that we serve a God who remains the same. He always has been. He is. And He will be forever. Our health will fail us. Relationships will grow stale. Finances will dry up. Businesses will close. But when we anchor our hope in God, we are securing ourselves to the only One who never changes. He is unaffected by the limitations we face. And we are beyond blessed to be loved by the Creator who gives us steadfast hope for eternal life and the beautiful things to come.

. . . .

Dear God, thank You for being a steady force in my life. Thank You for being predictably awesome. And thank You for being a safe place to anchor my heart. In the name of Jesus I pray. Amen.

YOU HAVE PERMANENT ACCESS

Our faith guarantees us permanent access into this marvelous kindness that has given us a perfect relationship with God. What incredible joy bursts forth within us as we keep on celebrating our hope of experiencing God's glory!

ROMANS 5:2 TPT

It's hard to imagine that we have permanent access to God. The one who created the heavens and the earth and everything in them is available to you right now and forevermore. And while we may forget to talk to God or try to go forward in our own strength, it doesn't change the truth that we have everlasting access to Him. Anytime we need the Lord, He is there. Ask God to make you keenly aware of His glory every day. Let Him be your first stop when things in life get gnarly.

· ·

Dear God, it's humbling to think someone like me has eternal access to someone like You. I'm deeply moved and blessed by Your enduring love. Help me never take it for granted. In the name of Jesus I pray. Amen.

79

GOD NEVER GROWS TIRED OR WEARY

Don't you know? Haven't you heard? The Eternal, the Everlasting God, the Creator of the whole world, never gets tired or weary. His wisdom is beyond understanding. God strengthens the weary and gives vitality to those worn down by age and care.
ISAIAH 40:28–29 VOICE

We may find ourselves worn out by the craziness of life, but God never tires. He doesn't grow weary at the barrage of life storms that come our way. The Lord is never confused or caught off guard. While we may buckle under the weight of worry, He sees the big picture and knows every detail and solution. And when we have reached the end of ourselves and are exhausted, it's God who will strengthen us for the next step. What a blessing that we don't have to master life on our own.

. . . .

Dear God, thank You for being big. Thank You for being all-powerful and all-knowing. And thank You for giving me what I need to navigate the ups and downs of life. In the name of Jesus I pray. Amen.

GOD WILL NEVER FAIL TO RESCUE

He will watch over his devoted lovers, never letting them
slip or be overthrown. He will send all my enemies to
the pit of destruction. Murderers, liars, and betrayers
will face an untimely death. My life's hope and trust
is in you, and you'll never fail to rescue me!
PSALM 55:23 TPT

How would you live differently if you were convinced that God would never fail to rescue you? Would it give you confidence to say yes to that project or to step out of your comfort zone and volunteer? Would you share your testimony? Would you live authentically, free to be yourself? God promises to watch over those who love Him. He will protect you from enemies. Friend, you're blessed to be loved in such a way. Your heavenly Father delights in who you are and promises to save.

. . . .

Dear God, anchor my hope and trust in You because
the Bible says You'll never fail to rescue me. Your
Word is true, and Your heart for me is always
good! In the name of Jesus I pray. Amen.

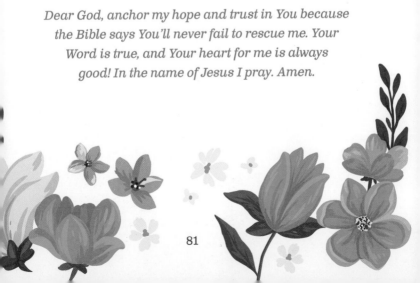

81

GOD IS YOUR SHEPHERD

*GOD, my shepherd! I don't need a thing. You have
bedded me down in lush meadows, you find me quiet
pools to drink from. True to your word, you let me
catch my breath and send me in the right direction.*
PSALM 23:1–3 MSG

Sometimes we just want someone else to make the decisions.
We want them to show us what to do. Our desire is for them
to guide us when we're confused and comfort us when we're
weary. Our hope is that they will not only anticipate our needs
but meet them with perfect timing and in the perfect way.
And we want them to point us in the right direction as their
confidence gives us peace. Be blessed knowing God is your
shepherd and He will fulfill every one of these hopes and
desires because He loves you.

* *

*Dear God, help me follow Your perfect paths for my
life. You know the ins and outs and ups and downs
ahead, and I can trust You to guide me into places
of peace. In the name of Jesus I pray. Amen.*

LET HIM QUIET YOUR FEAR

Even when your path takes me through the valley
of deepest darkness, fear will never conquer me,
for you already have! Your authority is my strength
and my peace. The comfort of your love takes away
my fear. I'll never be lonely, for you are near.

PSALM 23:4 TPT

For countless reasons, you are blessed to be a child of God. One of the most powerful is that being in a relationship with Him has the ability to quiet fear. So many of us walk around terrified of the future. We're afraid for our finances, our family, and our friends. And because fear has been with us for so long, it plays a part in every decision we make. But when we truly embrace our faith and put our trust in God, those dark valleys won't cause us to tremble. They won't rob us of joy. It's God's love that will bring comfort and keep us in that peaceful place only He can provide, regardless of the chaos swirling around us.

* *

Dear God, keep me in perfect peace.
In the name of Jesus I pray. Amen.

DINNER IN FRONT OF ENEMIES

You serve me a six-course dinner right in front of my enemies.
You revive my drooping head; my cup brims with blessing.
PSALM 23:5 MSG

What an extraordinary image. Visualize the Lord serving you a beautiful meal while your enemies watch. It's an unmatched display of favor and blessing. And this is why we can let God be the one to exact justice. It's why we can let Him be the judge on our behalf in full confidence. When we choose to stand in the shadow of the Most High and trust Him with our broken hearts, we will never be disappointed. Scripture says He will revive us; our sadness and heartbreak won't be forever. And in the end, we will be restored and blessed.

• •

Dear God, I confess I'm quick to point the finger in certain situations. But I'm resolved to press into my faith for the blessing that comes from letting You be the righteous Judge in all things. In the name of Jesus I pray. Amen.

THE GOD WHO PURSUES

So why would I fear the future? Only goodness and tender love pursue me all the days of my life. Then afterward, when my life is through, I'll return to your glorious presence to be forever with you!

PSALM 23:6 TPT

Did you know that every day the Lord pursues you? You matter so greatly, and that's why He makes you a priority for His love and attention. His desire is for you to pursue Him back, seeking community and comfort in your relationship. Friend, you are His beloved. Let this strengthen you and create courage. Let this breed confidence deep in your bones. There is no reason for you to fear or worry because God is with you always. He is actively pursuing you on earth, and at your final breath, He will be there to welcome you home with open arms.

· ·

Dear God, it makes me feel loved to know I'm worthy of Your pursuit. Thank You for never giving up on me! I want to be with You every day and forever. In the name of Jesus I pray. Amen.

A HEART OF GENEROSITY

So give generously to the person in need. Don't feel badly about this when you're doing it; because of your generosity, the Eternal your God will bless you in everything you do, in every project you begin.
DEUTERONOMY 15:10 VOICE

Some people were born with a heart of generosity. They are givers by nature. But others have to work on it a bit. Maybe they were raised by parents who were extremely frugal. Maybe fear grips them so they hold tightly to their resources. Or maybe they lack compassion for those hit by hard times. Regardless, God can cultivate a spirit of generosity in anyone. Ask Him to open your heart to others. Ask for that blessing so you can be a blessing to those around you.

* *

Dear God, open my eyes to see the needs of others. Let my heart be open as well. Use my time and resources as Your hands and feet to further the kingdom. Everything I have is Yours anyway! In the name of Jesus I pray. Amen.

OVERWHELMED WITH BLESSINGS

But I will say this to encourage your generosity: the one who plants little harvests little, and the one who plants plenty harvests plenty. . . . God is ready to overwhelm you with more blessings than you could ever imagine so that you'll always be taken care of in every way and you'll have more than enough to share.

2 CORINTHIANS 9:6, 8 VOICE

Scripture says you reap what you sow, so let this be a challenge to cultivate a big heart—because when you bless little, you get little blessings back. But when you're extravagant with your kindness, it comes back to you in kind. Friend, be excited to live openhanded with your life. Lavish love on those around you. Look for ways to be abundant in your relationships. And know that when you live generously, God sees it. Even more than that, He'll overwhelm you with blessings.

. . . .

Dear God, I want my life to be marked by generosity. Grow in me a deep compassion and use me for kingdom work. In the name of Jesus I pray. Amen.

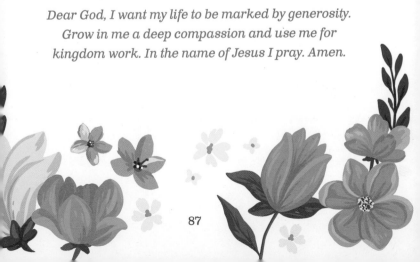

87

GIVING BLESSES YOU MOST

"I've left you an example of how you should serve and take care of those who are weak. For we must always cherish the words of our Lord Jesus, who taught, 'Giving brings a far greater blessing than receiving.'"
ACTS 20:35 TPT

Ask God to bless you with a deep love for others, because it's out of that love we cultivate a servant's heart. Part of that means we learn to be—and eventually desire to be—givers. We are generous with our time. We're givers of our treasure. We become encouragers to the weary of spirit. And at the end of the day, what we want most is to meet a need and be a support for those who need a boost. But the most amazing part is that when we choose to give, it blesses us the most. Isn't God magnificent?

. . . .

Dear God, I'm in awe of You. I am blown away by Your ways. Who ever thought giving would bless the giver the most? I just love You! In the name of Jesus I pray. Amen.

88

WHEN YOU SEEK TO PLEASE

To those who seek to please God, He gives wisdom and knowledge and joyfulness; but to those who are wicked, God keeps them busy harvesting and storing up for those in whom He delights. But even this is fleeting; it's like trying to embrace the wind.
ECCLESIASTES 2:26 VOICE

When you make it a priority to follow after God in the way you live your life, blessings will abound. That's just the way God works. Making the hard choices you know will glorify Him—rather than the easy choices that glorify your flesh—delights the Father. And it's because of your obedience that He deposits wisdom and knowledge and joy in your heart. These aren't things you will have to look for or work for. These are blessings poured out because of your faith-filled decisions.

· ·

Dear God, I'm grateful that You honor us in such beautiful ways. I appreciate the blessings You so freely give. Help me always chase hard after You. In the name of Jesus I pray. Amen.

THE LAST PART

The Eternal One blessed the last part of Job's life even more
than the first part. He went on to possess 14,000 sheep, 6,000
camels, 1,000 teams of oxen, and 1,000 female donkeys.
He also fathered 7 more sons and 3 more daughters.
JOB 42:12–13 VOICE

Let today's scripture wash over you. Who doesn't need a reminder that we are never too old to receive blessings? The truth is that the more we age, the more opportunities we've had to lose those things important to us. There have been more valleys and hilltops because we've had more years in the journey. And while many of us have lost so much, Job's story can lift our spirits as we realize just like him that God may bless the last part of our lives too. It's never too late to experience the beauty of a life of faith. So cling to the Lord, open your eyes, and watch for the blessings!

* * *

Dear God, what a great reminder that Your
blessings come in different ways and at any age!
Thank You! In the name of Jesus I pray. Amen.

PLANS FOR GOOD

Joseph replied, "Don't be afraid. Do I act for God? Don't you see, you planned evil against me but God used those same plans for my good, as you see all around you right now—life for many people. Easy now, you have nothing to fear; I'll take care of you and your children." He reassured them, speaking with them heart-to-heart.
GENESIS 50:19–21 MSG

What a blessing to know God can take the enemy's evil plans and use them for our benefit. There is no one on earth who has that kind of control. No one in our circle loves us with that kind of ferocity. There isn't a person here who has the power and reach to orchestrate things in such a way. Your faith is a shield that covers you deep in God's love and protects you from what the enemy meant to discourage or destroy you.

· ·

Dear God, I don't always know when You're reworking the enemy's plans on my behalf, but I am so grateful! Thank You for loving me with such ferocity! In the name of Jesus I pray. Amen.

91

WHEN IT'S TIME TO MOVE

*GOD told Abram: "Leave your country, your family,
and your father's home for a land that I will show
you. I'll make you a great nation and bless you. I'll
make you famous; you'll be a blessing. I'll bless those
who bless you; those who curse you I'll curse. All the
families of the Earth will be blessed through you."*

GENESIS 12:1–3 MSG

Sometimes God tells us to stay put and grow where He's planted us. But other times His plan is for us to go. It could be a physical move to another town in your state, or it could be a move across the country. Maybe it's a change from one company to another. It may even be stepping out of your comfort zone, taking a step in a new direction in life. Regardless, when you decide to obey, God will bless you for it. Be sensitive to God's leading because His plan is well thought out and tailored for you.

. . . .

*Dear God, I will go when You tell me to
go. In the name of Jesus I pray. Amen.*

YOU ARE A LIGHT

You are like that illuminating light. Let your light shine everywhere you go, that you may illumine creation, so men and women everywhere may see your good actions, may see creation at its fullest, may see your devotion to Me, and may turn and praise your Father in heaven because of it.
MATTHEW 5:16 VOICE

We have the opportunity to shine a spotlight on God with how we choose to live our lives. Make no mistake, people are always watching. And we can bless Him by living in honest ways and being willing to share our faith journey with others. It's how we shine a light. It's how we *are* a light in this world. When we're intentional with words and actions, our belief can point others to God. When we live the blessed life God intended, He can use us to bless others.

· ·

Dear God, let my life shine a spotlight on Your faithfulness! Help me be aware that the words I say and the way I live preaches to those around me. In the name of Jesus I pray. Amen.

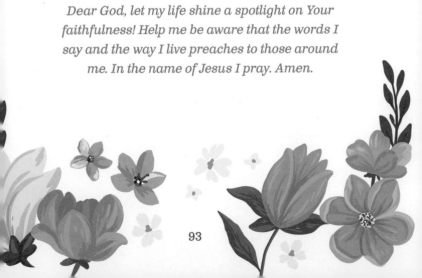

93

OVERWHELMED BY GOD'S GOODNESS

*We laughed and laughed and overflowed with
gladness. We were left shouting for joy and singing
your praise. All the nations saw it and joined in, saying,
"The Lord has done great miracles for them!" Yes,
he did mighty miracles and we are overjoyed!*

PSALM 126:2–3 TPT

Sometimes all we can do when we witness a blessing is laugh. When we see God move in unanticipated ways, sometimes our only response is shouting for joy or breaking into song. Have you ever been overwhelmed by God's goodness? Have you ever seen healing or restoration in unexpected places? Don't be shy. God loves it when we praise Him demonstratively. Raise a hallelujah for fresh provision, open doors, new contacts, extended grace, or softened hearts. Let Him know you see the blessing and thank Him for it.

. . . .

*Dear God, open my eyes to see the ways You bless
me and those I love. You are the greatest gift giver
ever! In the name of Jesus I pray. Amen.*

94

WIDE, OPEN SPACES

When trouble surrounded me, I cried out to the Eternal;
He answered me and brought me to a wide, open space.
The Eternal is with me, so I will not be afraid of anything.
If God is on my side, how can anyone hurt me?
PSALM 118:5–6 VOICE

To be in a wide, open space means to be free of the pressures that create stress and worry and fear. Can you remember a time when it felt like you were surrounded by chaos? It was as if the weight of the world was sitting on your chest. It was hard to get a good, deep breath because things felt so heavy. Scripture tells us that when we're in this kind of situation, we can cry out to God. Not only will He hear us, but He will bless us with freedom. And in His sovereignty, God will create space so we can find our footing and strengthen our faith.

• •

Dear God, thank You for the beautiful blessing of wide,
open spaces! In the name of Jesus I pray. Amen.

95

HE WILL DO IT AGAIN

Now, Lord, do it again! Restore us to our former glory!
May streams of your refreshing flow over us until our dry
hearts are drenched again. Those who sow their tears
as seeds will reap a harvest with joyful shouts of glee.

PSALM 126:4–5 TPT

The gift of restoration is a powerful blessing that comes only from the Lord. He has a way of refreshing the stale and musty places in our hearts. He can breathe new life into a relationship that's crumbling. God can renew our hope and joy, bringing peace back into a situation that feels too overwhelming. And the most amazing part is that He will do it again and again. There is no end to His love for you. Every time you need restoration, all you have to do is ask.

• •

Dear God, You are so kind and generous to the
faithful. Thank You for the blessing of restoration,
giving it freely and fully when asked. You're a good,
good Father. In the name of Jesus I pray. Amen.

96

TAKE REFUGE IN GOD

*GOD's my strong champion; I flick off my enemies like
flies. Far better to take refuge in GOD than trust in people;
far better to take refuge in GOD than trust in celebrities.*
PSALM 118:7–9 MSG

When it comes right down to it, our best bet is to take refuge
in God. Chances are you have amazing friends and a loving,
caring family, but they cannot do what He can do in your life.
They cannot save you like He can save you. They cannot love
you like He can love you. They cannot bless you in the ways
He can. When you anchor every hope to what the world can
offer—even when its intentions are good—you will be let down
in the end. Let God be your strong champion in life because
there is no one and nothing that can compare.

. . . .

*Dear God, I am blessed by Your love and compassion
for me. Remind me that You are my strong champion
and that taking refuge in You is always the best
choice. In the name of Jesus I pray. Amen.*

REPAYING BAD
WITH A BLESSING

*Finally, all of you, be like-minded and show sympathy,
love, compassion, and humility to and for each other—
not paying back evil with evil or insult with insult, but
repaying the bad with a blessing. It was this you were
called to do, so that you might inherit a blessing.*

1 PETER 3:8–9 VOICE

It's hard to imagine having the strength to repay bad with a
blessing. So why do we do it? Because it brings blessings back
on us. And, more importantly, because God is calling us to live
that way. So rather than mouth off in response to someone who
verbally berates you, keep your mouth shut. When you want to
expose someone's secrets because they've gossiped about your
painful situation, pray for them instead. When you're tempted to
set someone up to fail because they have deeply hurt you, walk
away. God is asking you to be sympathetic, compassionate, and
humble toward everyone. And He will bless you for it.

. . . .

*Dear God, give me the strength to repay bad with
a blessing. In the name of Jesus I pray. Amen.*

A GENEROUS SPIRIT

*When you are generous to the poor, you
are enriched with blessings in return.*

PROVERBS 22:9 TPT

There are a million reasons to be stingy and selfish, but none of them are valid according to the Lord. He's challenging us to be generous to others, to be caring and compassionate. His desire is for us to live at peace whenever possible. Rather than encourage an eye-for-an-eye mentality, God incentivizes us to live with a kind heart toward the poor. Sometimes that's a hard choice, but there's a blessing that comes from it. Not only does our generous spirit come from God, but it's also rewarded by God. If you're struggling to find a generous spirit, ask for His help. He will make it so.

· ·

*Dear God, make my heart tender toward those who
are struggling in any way. Let me live with kindness
and generosity knowing it delights You! And thank
You for blessing obedience. Lord, You really do think
of everything. In the name of Jesus I pray. Amen.*

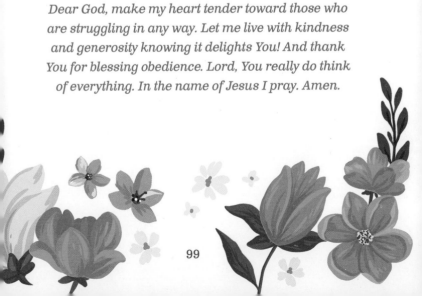

99

THE GOD WHO KNOWS YOU

You see all things; You saw me growing, changing in my mother's womb; every detail of my life was already written in Your book; You established the length of my life before I ever tasted the sweetness of it.

PSALM 139:16 VOICE

What a blessing to understand there is unmatched depth to God's knowledge of who we are. To realize He watched us grow in our mothers' bellies is breathtaking. To learn He knows every detail of our lives because He planned them helps us trust His leading. And today's verse allows us to take comfort in knowing our breaths have been determined from our birth to our passing into eternity. Friend, that means we can live with a sense of peace because we have a God who cares for us and has gone before us. There is no greater blessing.

* *

Dear God, what a privilege to be known and seen by You. Let my heart register this beautiful blessing every day, and let it bring me unshakable peace. In the name of Jesus I pray. Amen.

SURROUNDED AND TRAPPED

Yes, they surrounded me, like a swarm of killer bees swirling around me. I was trapped like one trapped by a raging fire; I was surrounded with no way out and at the point of collapse. But by Yahweh's supernatural power, I overcame them all!
PSALM 118:11–12 TPT

Every single one of us has felt surrounded and trapped. Chances are you've been in situations where it seemed the walls were closing in. You felt out of options. You lacked solid solutions. We've all faced circumstances where we couldn't see a way out. The common thread in these moments is fear, and God is the only chance we've got. Be blessed knowing He sees your struggle and has already made a way for victory. Be quick to ask the Lord for rescue and restoration.

. . . .

Dear God, thank You for making me a priority. Thank You for knowing me and pulling me from enemy chaos. What a blessing to realize that when I feel surrounded and trapped, You are there to help. In the name of Jesus I pray. Amen.

STICKING WITH GOD

"But blessed is the man who trusts me, GOD, the woman who sticks with GOD. They're like trees replanted in Eden, putting down roots near the rivers—never a worry through the hottest of summers, never dropping a leaf, serene and calm through droughts, bearing fresh fruit every season."

JEREMIAH 17:7–8 MSG

Scripture says that you're blessed if you trust God. So what does blessed look like? Maybe it's a new job or a promotion. Maybe it's a sense of peace where there has been stress. Maybe it's a restored relationship or closing the door on an unhealthy one. Regardless, when we press into God for strength and guidance and help, it is rewarded through God's intervention. Friend, be the kind of woman who sticks with God through the valleys and mountains of life. Let your roots of faith go deep.

· ·

Dear God, I want to be filled with faith in You no matter the situation I'm facing. I want to know deep in my heart that trusting You will yield powerful results. Help me stand strong in my belief of Your goodness! In the name of Jesus I pray. Amen.

102

RIGHT ON THE EDGE

They pushed me right up to the edge, and I was ready
to fall, but you helped me to triumph, and together we
overcame them all. Lord, you are my true strength
and my glory-song, my champion, my Savior!
PSALM 118:13–14 TPT

Life is so challenging. Sometimes we can't help but feel like we're standing right on the edge, ready to tumble into an abyss where we won't be able to find our way back. It could be a financial struggle, a frustrating relationship, a health scare, or insecurities and fears we have faced for years. There are daily circumstances that threaten to leave us feeling hopeless. Let today's scripture be a blessing and encouragement to know God will catch us before we fall. It's through His help we will be overcomers. It's okay when you don't feel strong because the Lord is your true strength!

. . . .

Dear God, do You see me on the edge right now? I'm
overwhelmed and unable to navigate my situation
without You. Please come quick and bless me by being
my champion. In the name of Jesus I pray. Amen.

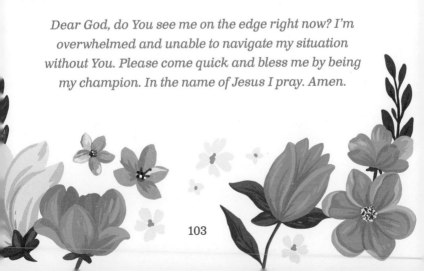

103

EVEN MORE BLESSED

*Jesus commented, "Even more blessed are those
who hear God's Word and guard it with their lives!"*
LUKE 11:28 MSG

Be honest… How many times have you heard a powerful sermon, resolved to make changes in your life, and by dinnertime had already forgotten the words that moved you earlier? Have you ever heard a fabulous speaker who challenged you to a higher level of faith, and that desire to step up began to wane as you backed out of the parking lot? Don't miss the gold nugget in today's scripture! While we are blessed to hear the Word of God, we're *even more* blessed when we guard it. Every time you choose His way over yours, it will be honored. Each moment you walk out His will rather than follow what's trending in the world, God will recognize it. Don't miss your opportunity for a double portion of blessings—because there is nothing more powerful than what God can give.

* *

*Dear God, help me guard Your Word in my heart
every day! In the name of Jesus I pray. Amen.*

PRAISING GOD FOR HIS BLESSINGS

I have found the gateway to God, the pathway to his presence for all his devoted lovers. I will offer all my loving praise to you, and I thank you so much for answering my prayer and bringing me salvation!

PSALM 118:20–21 TPT

Most of the time we are so focused on asking God for help or strength that we forget to praise Him. In our desperation, we become laser focused on our lack and don't see our abundance. We get stuck in the rut of sharing a laundry list of hopes without recognizing when those requests are answered. It's so important that we're intentional to thank God for the ways He has blessed us. It not only delights His heart, but it also keeps us focused on His goodness and love. And now, as ever, we need to be reminded of how God has showed up in our lives. Make time to bless the Lord for blessing you!

. . . .

Dear God, thank You! In the name of Jesus I pray. Amen.

105

A BLESSING FOR YOUR TRUST

Bow down before God's son. If you don't, you will face His anger and retribution, and you won't stand a chance. For it doesn't take long to kindle royal wrath, but blessings await all who trust in Him. They will find God a gentle refuge.

PSALM 2:12 VOICE

Where do you need to trust God today? Are you worried about your child's struggle with friends? Are you concerned about the meeting with your employer next week? Is the deadline quickly approaching and you haven't made a decision? Are you anxious about the state of a relationship? The problem is that when we stew in our struggles and don't surrender them to God, we get all tangled up. But there's a blessing waiting for you, and your faith is the ticket to collect it. Choose to trust God and let Him be your refuge.

* *

Dear God, help me surrender control and trust You with my life. I want the blessing that comes from it. In the name of Jesus I pray. Amen.

THIS VERY DAY

This is the very day of the Lord that brings gladness and joy, filling our hearts with glee. O God, please come and save us again; bring us your breakthrough-victory!
PSALM 118:24–25 TPT

This very day—and every day, actually—we can find gladness and joy and glee. Even in the hardest seasons and the darkest valleys, when we cling to the Lord we will be able to access these things. And they can bless us and refocus our weary hearts. We will still grieve and struggle, but joy can coexist. It won't be joy for our difficult situation, but joy because we know God will bring breakthrough-victory in the right way at the right time. It gives us an anchor to tie hope to. And it's the greatest of blessings.

. . . .

Dear God, I am watching for the breakthrough-victory brought through my faith in You. It's in Your magnificent love that You will save me again. Help me have joy and gladness as I wait in expectation. In the name of Jesus I pray. Amen.

107

THE MOST EPIC BLESSING EVER

"The Son of Man is ready to be lifted up, so that those who truly believe in him will not perish but be given eternal life. For here is the way God loved the world—he gave his only, unique Son as a gift. So now everyone who believes in him will never perish but experience everlasting life."

JOHN 3:14–16 TPT

The biggest, most epic blessing you'll ever receive is Jesus. There's nothing anyone can do for you, there's nothing anyone can give you, and there's nothing you can earn that will come close to His sacrifice on the cross. He stepped out of heaven and into a sin-filled world so your trespasses could no longer keep you from community with God. It's exclusively because of His Son and your faith that you'll not perish but live in eternity with the Lord. Thank Him every day!

. . . .

Dear God, thank You for Jesus! Somehow those words don't feel weighty enough for the blessing He's given me, but I recognize it's His finished work on the cross that's sealed my eternity with You. In the name of Jesus I pray. Amen.

GOD'S LOVE NEVER QUITS

Blessed are you who enter in GOD's name—from GOD's house we bless you! GOD is God, he has bathed us in light. Adorn the shrine with garlands, hang colored banners above the altar! You're my God, and I thank you. O my God, I lift high your praise. Thank GOD—he's so good. His love never quits!
PSALM 118:26–29 MSG

In a world where love fails us on the regular, what a breath of fresh air to take in today's scripture. To know God's love doesn't quit is a beautiful promise we can't overlook or take for granted. It means that even in our wretchedness, He sees the good in us. When we are rebellious and disobedient, His love never wavers. When we become faithful followers, God looks at us through the cleansing blood of Jesus. And no matter what, His love can never be compromised! Meditate on that truth today and let your praises rise to the heavens.

. . . .

Dear God, what a blessing to know Your love will never give up on me! In the name of Jesus I pray. Amen.

109

THE END OF CONDEMNATION

"God did not send his Son into the world to judge and condemn the world, but to be its Savior and rescue it! So now there is no longer any condemnation for those who believe in him, but the unbeliever already lives under condemnation because they do not believe in the name of the only Son of God."

JOHN 3:17–18 TPT

Many of us live with condemning feelings every day. It may be something we sense from others for who we are or how we live our lives, or it might be something we put on ourselves. Regardless, it's exhausting to walk around with shame and guilt on our shoulders. Friend, one of the most powerful blessings we receive when we choose Jesus to be our Savior is the end of condemnation. Our belief in the Lord, if we allow it, will flush away those feelings of shame and guilt. We can live in the freedom Christ brought to those who have faith in Him!

• •

Dear God, help me embrace freedom over condemnation every time! In the name of Jesus I pray. Amen.

POURING OF HIS BLESSING

To rectify this situation, you must bring the entire tithe into the storage house in the temple so that there may be food for Me and for the Levites in My house. Feel free to test Me now in this. See whether or not I, the Eternal, Commander of heavenly armies, will open the windows of heaven to you and pour a blessing down upon you until all needs are satisfied.

MALACHI 3:10 VOICE

Malachi 3:10 brings up a tricky topic because it has to do with money, but it's scripture, so we can't ignore it. We're challenged to test God. He's saying when we commit to tithing, it opens heaven's storehouse of blessings. This is once again an example of God recognizing our obedience and pouring out His goodness in response. It's a powerful concept we see threaded throughout His Word! And because we know God is incapable of lying or changing His mind, we can believe this blessing to be true.

. . . .

Dear God, give me the confidence to walk this out. In the name of Jesus I pray. Amen.

111

THE LIGHT

"So the wicked hate the Light and try to hide from it, for the Light fully exposes their lives. But those who love the truth will come into the Light, for the Light will reveal that it was God who produced their fruitful works."

JOHN 3:20–21 TPT

It's all about the Lord. We may think it's about us. We may get caught up in what this world offers. We may focus on all the wrong things for hope and help. But when we embrace the Lord—the light—we will find the truth we desperately need. Make no mistake, the blessings we have in our lives are from God. He is the one who *gives* us good things. It's through Him we are able to *do* good things. And He is the one who supplies us with everything we need to walk out the call He has thoughtfully placed on our lives. The Lord is the light of the world, and we are richly blessed by Him.

Dear God, fill my life with Your light!
In the name of Jesus I pray. Amen.

PRAISING GOD FOR IT ALL

Give thanks to GOD—he is good and his love never quits.
Say, "Save us, Savior God, round us up and get us out
of these godless places, so we can give thanks to your
holy Name, and bask in your life of praise." Blessed be
GOD, the God of Israel, from everlasting to everlasting.
Then everybody said, "Yes! Amen!" and "Praise GOD!"
1 CHRONICLES 16:34–36 MSG

Have you ever prayed for God to get you out of a godless place?
Have you ever muttered the words *"Come, Lord Jesus"*? We
can praise Him because we know He is the one who will save
us in the end. He is the one who will bring the rescue. God is
the one who will anchor us through the storm. And He is the
one to praise for His unwavering goodness and unshakable
love! Friend, you are blessed as a child of God. Let that truth
keep you warm.

. . . .

Dear God, I praise You for who You are and all You have
done. Thank You! In the name of Jesus I pray. Amen.

YOU ARE WHO YOU HANG OUT WITH

If you want to grow in wisdom, spend time with the wise. Walk with the wicked and you'll eventually become just like them. Calamity chases the sin-chaser, but prosperity pursues the God-lover.
PROVERBS 13:20–21 TPT

The truth is you are who you hang out with. You will begin to pick up the mannerisms of the ones you spend your time around. You will begin to believe what they believe and act the way they act. So let today's scripture remind you to surround yourself with the right people. People can either bless you or curse you. Time spent with them will change you one way or the other. If you want to grow in your relationship with God, make choices that reflect your faith, be filled with love and compassion for others, and then spend time with those who want the same.

* * *

Dear God, help me be mindful of the company I keep. I want to thrive in a community that puts You first. Bless me with the right friends. In the name of Jesus I pray. Amen.

114

THE BLESSING OF LIBERATION

*Therefore, now no condemnation awaits those who
are living in Jesus the Anointed, the Liberating King,
because when you live in the Anointed One, Jesus, a new
law takes effect. The law of the Spirit of life breathes into
you and liberates you from the law of sin and death.*

ROMANS 8:1–2 VOICE

When you anchor your faith in God, everything changes. You're
a different person living under a different law, and it's the law of
liberty. Without being covered by the blood of Jesus, you are still
subject to the penalty of sin. There has been no reconciliation
on your behalf. But when you understand the blessing of Jesus
and accept His gift of salvation, you are forgiven and renewed.
Every sin with your name on it has been settled up and paid
for. The King has liberated you.

* *

*Dear God, thank You for the new law that took effect when
I chose Jesus as my Savior. What a beautiful blessing.
Let me be intentional to live every day in the freedom You
have given me. In the name of Jesus I pray. Amen.*

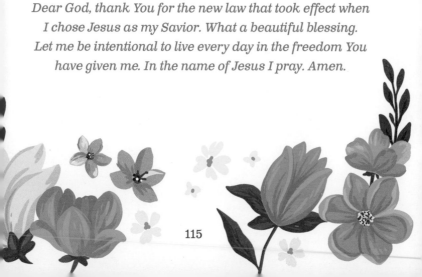

CHILD OF GOD

He came to the people he created—to those who should
have received him, but they did not recognize him. But
those who embraced him and took hold of his name
he gave authority to become the children of God!
JOHN 1:11–12 TPT

What a blessing that we may be called children of God! We can't earn that privilege or manipulate anything to get it. We don't have to look a certain way or live in a certain place. Our politics won't bring it about, nor will our daily habits influence it. Instead, scripture tells us that when we embrace the Lord for who He is and accept Him as our personal Savior, that powerful act of faith gives us the title of God's child. There is no greater identity for us! Every day, let's choose to recognize the blessings that come from it.

. . . .

Dear God, there is no greater gift than knowing I am Your
child. Thank You for choosing me! Let me live every day in
Your strength and power. In the name of Jesus I pray. Amen.

GOD WON'T LET GO

"Every person the Father gives me eventually comes running to me. And once that person is with me, I hold on and don't let go. I came down from heaven not to follow my own agenda but to accomplish the will of the One who sent me."
JOHN 6:37–38 MSG

Let it be a blessing to your heart to know the Lord will never let go of you. No matter what battles you face in relationships, He will surround you with His presence. Regardless of the bad and overwhelming news that comes, you will be held tight. Every time your foundation feels unstable, He will hold your feet steady. God will never find a reason to release those who love Him. He won't even look for one. Let that truth comfort your weary heart today. You are His forever!

. . . .

Dear God, hold me close and don't give up on me. Remind me of the blessing of Your constant presence, especially when I'm battling fear and insecurity. In the name of Jesus I pray. Amen.

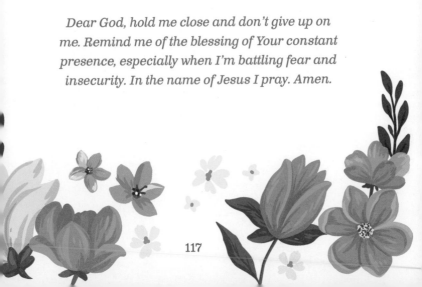

WE CANNOT BE SNATCHED FROM HIS HAND

"I give to them the gift of eternal life and they will never be lost and no one has the power to snatch them out of my hands. My Father, who has given them to me as his gift, is the mightiest of all, and no one has the power to snatch them from my Father's care."

JOHN 10:28-29 TPT

In the last reading, we talked about the powerful truth that God will not let us go. Today, let's embrace the second part of that blessing, which is that no one and nothing can snatch us from His hands. The Lord promises to keep us forever without compromise, and His Word never fails. That means we are secure in Him no matter what. And there's no circumstance, incident, or person that can change that fact. We can take comfort in His promise and live with confidence of His love!

. . . .

Dear God, I love how possessive You are of Your children. What a blessing to know that once I'm Yours, nothing can change it. Thank You for loving me fully and completely! In the name of Jesus I pray. Amen.

118

THE SPIRIT'S CONSTANT COMPANIONSHIP

I will ask the Father to send you another Helper, the Spirit of truth, who will remain constantly with you. The world does not recognize the Spirit of truth, because it does not know the Spirit and is unable to receive Him. But you do know the Spirit because He lives with you, and He will dwell in you.

JOHN 14:16–17 VOICE

Let's touch on one more beautiful truth about God's unwavering love. We've already learned that He will not let go of us and that no one can snatch us from His hands. Today we're reminded that His Holy Spirit will be our constant companion. Friend, there may be times you feel alone and abandoned. You may feel rejected by others. But be blessed in knowing that God is with you. Always. You are fully known, fully seen, and fully loved. Forever.

• •

Dear God, thank You for being so clear in Your Word about Your unwavering presence in my life. Honestly, I needed a reminder. In the name of Jesus I pray. Amen.

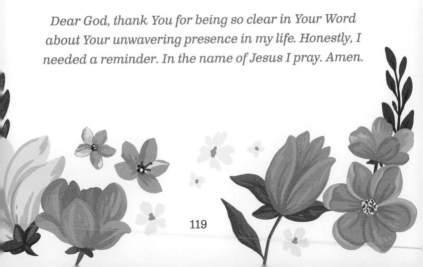

FAITH OF ABRAHAM

He never stopped believing God's promise, for he was made strong in his faith to father a child. And because he was mighty in faith and convinced that God had all the power needed to fulfill his promises, Abraham glorified God!
ROMANS 4:20–21 TPT

There's no doubt Abraham was a faithful follower of God! He was not perfect, but he lived with purpose to do what the Lord asked of him. And in return, God blessed him mightily. Abraham's faith was so strong that he was completely convinced God would fill in the gaps of his limitations. His belief gave him confidence and the courage to take the next step in God's plan. Today, ask the Lord to bless you with the faith of Abraham and be empowered to live with radical belief in God's abilities through you!

. . . .

Dear God, thank You for the example of Abraham in the Bible. Bless me with his unshakable belief so I can navigate life with confidence and strength, knowing You will always come through for me. In the name of Jesus I pray. Amen.

IN OUR SINFULNESS

So if while we were still enemies, God fully reconciled us to himself through the death of his Son, then something greater than friendship is ours. Now that we are at peace with God, and because we share in his resurrection life, how much more we will be rescued from sin's dominion!

ROMANS 5:10 TPT

It's one thing to be kind to others when they are kind first. We may be able to respond with compassion to someone who's agreeable. But friend, it's a whole different ball game to act in generosity toward those who are wretched and offensive. They're the ones we'd want to turn our backs on and walk away from in disgust. Understand that this was our state as mankind when God sent Jesus to reconcile us through His death on the cross. Jesus chose to die to save us in our sinfulness. Let that blessed reality wash over you today, and find a moment to thank God for the depth of His love.

. . . .

Dear God, I'm humbled by Your compassion and grateful for Your love. In the name of Jesus I pray. Amen.

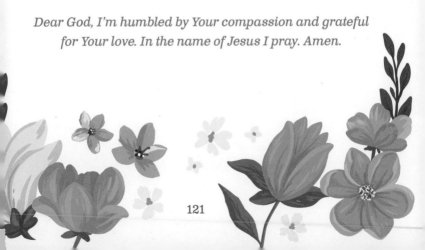

121

CLEARING AWAY OUR SINS

This is how God showed his love for us: God sent his only Son into the world so we might live through him. This is the kind of love we are talking about—not that we once upon a time loved God, but that he loved us and sent his Son as a sacrifice to clear away our sins and the damage they've done to our relationship with God.
1 JOHN 4:9–10 MSG

How do you try to conceal your sins? How do you cover up the damage left behind because of your wrong choices? There's no doubt we look for ways to clean up our mistakes. And it's often our shame and guilt that drive us to camouflage and mask our mess-ups. But friend, let's recognize the blessing we were given through Jesus' death on the cross, because that beautiful and selfless act removed our sin—past, present, and future. You don't need to cover up your transgressions, because they've been cleared away by His blood.

* *

Dear God, thank You.
In the name of Jesus I pray. Amen.

KNOWN BEFORE BIRTH

For he knew all about us before we were born and he destined us from the beginning to share the likeness of his Son. This means the Son is the oldest among a vast family of brothers and sisters who will become just like him.

ROMANS 8:29 TPT

God has known about you since before you were even born. Every detail was worked out by your Creator. He was the one to determine the color of your eyes and hair and how tall you'd grow to be. He knew the exact day you would make your grand entrance into the world. And God crafted you, delighting in the beautiful plan He had for your life. The next time you feel insignificant or misunderstood, remember that the Lord has taken a very personal interest in all things *you*. He knows your value and your heart. Be blessed by that truth.

. . . .

Dear God, it's mind-blowing to think You knew me before I took my first breath. To know You were involved in my creation overwhelms me. I'm humbled. In the name of Jesus I pray. Amen.

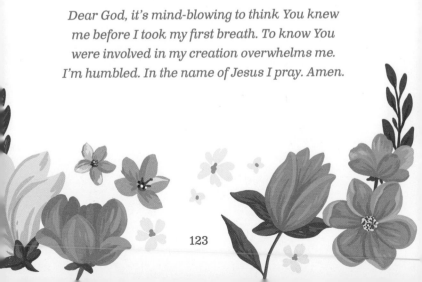

HE WON'T CONDEMN

Who then is left to condemn us? Certainly not Jesus, the Anointed One! For he gave his life for us, and even more than that, he has conquered death and is now risen, exalted, and enthroned by God at his right hand. So how could he possibly condemn us since he is continually praying for our triumph?

ROMANS 8:34 TPT

We may feel condemnation from family or friends for staying true to what we believe. We might feel judged by coworkers or neighbors for how we live. We may even feel criticized by other parents who are raising their kids differently. The truth is we will face those condemning folks throughout our lives, but the Lord will never be one of them. We might feel convicted—encouraged, even—through the Holy Spirit to change our lives to better align with His will, but we'll never feel attacked by God.

. . . .

Dear God, I'm blessed by knowing those feelings of doom and gloom are not from You. Remind me that You'll always call me higher, but it will never cause me to feel beat up. In the name of Jesus I pray. Amen.

INSEPARABLE

*So who can separate us? What can come between
us and the love of God's Anointed? Can troubles,
hardships, persecution, hunger, poverty, danger,
or even death? The answer is, absolutely nothing.*

ROMANS 8:35 VOICE

We live in a world filled with broken things. That's just the nature of a fallen world. We will all face broken relationships. Our financial security will strain and crumble from time to time. Our health will eventually break down. And some of our dreams may wash away. But have hope! For there is nothing that can come between you and God. Nothing will deteriorate the love He has for you. Friend, nothing has the power to separate you from Him. Let that bless your broken heart today.

• •

*Dear God, I'm encouraged today. I sometimes feel hopeless
because things around me seem so unstable. Thank
You for the reminder that You and I are inseparable. No
matter what I do, no matter what I say, no matter what is
happening in my world, the blessing of Your presence will
be with me forever. In the name of Jesus I pray. Amen.*

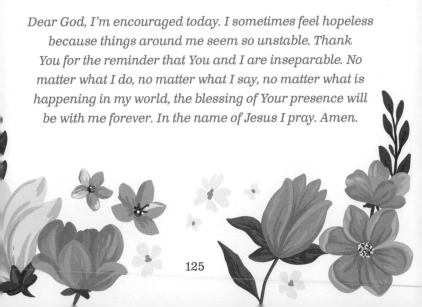

125

WHEN WE NEED CONFIDENCE

*I have every confidence that nothing—not death,
life, heavenly messengers, dark spirits, the present,
the future, spiritual powers, height, depth, nor any
created thing—can come between us and the love of
God revealed in the Anointed, Jesus our Lord.*
ROMANS 8:38–39 VOICE

We cannot be separated from God. There is nothing earthly or heavenly that can come between us and the Lord. That is a big relief and an even bigger blessing. The problem is sometimes we lack the confidence to hold on to that truth. Ask the Lord to increase your faith so you can cling to this promise with fervor, never letting it shake or wobble when you are struggling. Let this blessing of hope be your anchor in the storm.

. . . .

*Dear God, give me the confidence my soul lacks.
I want the blessing of Your truth. Increase my
faith today. In the name of Jesus I pray. Amen.*

NO TAKE BACKS

When God chooses someone and graciously
imparts gifts to him, they are never rescinded.
ROMANS 11:29 TPT

When God gives you something, it's for keeps. Every gift you receive from your heavenly Father has a purpose that cannot be taken away. In His infinite wisdom, He chooses the right blessings for the right people at the right time. When you need strength for the journey ahead, you will receive it. When you need wisdom to choose wisely, it will be imparted. When you need peace to navigate the chaos, expect it to be given. When your circumstances call for patience or endurance, it is on its way. By faith, respond to each gift with confidence, being grateful that God's blessings are power-packed and yours to keep.

. . . .

Dear God, thank You for choosing me and trusting me
with Your gracious gifts. Help me not only see them but
use them with wisdom. Show me how to steward each
one with integrity. In the name of Jesus I pray. Amen.

127

RIGHT IN FRONT OF YOU

Just think—you don't need a thing, you've got it all! All God's gifts are right in front of you as you wait expectantly for our Master Jesus to arrive on the scene for the Finale. And not only that, but God himself is right alongside to keep you steady and on track until things are all wrapped up by Jesus.

1 CORINTHIANS 1:7–8 MSG

You're never alone in the battle. Though you may feel alone at times, God is with you always. And when you feel weak—worried you don't have what it takes—remember that because of the Lord, you don't need a thing. Scripture says all His gifts are right in front of you, so take what you need. Is it discernment? Joy? Forgiveness? Humility? Hope? Friend, don't give in to the lie of the enemy that says you are by yourself. Cry out to God and watch as His blessings fall on you.

. . . .

Dear God, thank You for knowing exactly what I need and providing it exactly when I need it. In the name of Jesus I pray. Amen.

THE SAME LOVE

It was always in his perfect plan to adopt us as his delightful children, through our union with Jesus, the Anointed One, so that his tremendous love that cascades over us would glorify his grace—for the same love he has for the Beloved, Jesus, he has for us. And this unfolding plan brings him great pleasure!

EPHESIANS 1:5–6 TPT

Can you believe that the same love God has for His Son, Jesus, He has for you too? That should bless your socks off, friend. Truthfully, it may feel overwhelming to the most seasoned saint and the new Christian alike. It feels surreal. But because of Jesus, we now have a way to become adopted as His beloved. It was His perfect plan all along. And we are the ones blessed by God's tremendous love and Jesus' sacrifice!

. . . .

Dear God, I'm humbled to be loved in the same way You love Your Son. Let that powerful truth sink deep into my heart today. In the name of Jesus I pray. Amen.

129

THE DEPTH OF GOD'S LOVE

But God still loved us with such great love. He is so rich
in compassion and mercy. Even when we were dead
and doomed in our many sins, he united us into the very
life of Christ and saved us by his wonderful grace!
EPHESIANS 2:4–5 TPT

It's hard to get our minds to wrap around how much God loves us. We read in His Word about the depth of His compassion for His children. We listen to sermons unpacking scripture that points to this truth. We sing songs of praise, thanking the Lord for His unshakable love. But do we truly grasp the depth of this blessing? Are we fully embracing the way our Creator feels about us? Meditate on today's scripture and ask God to make His love come alive in your heart. Ask Him to make you profoundly aware of how much He cares. And then choose to believe it in faith.

. . . .

Dear God, open my eyes to see Your love in all its glory.
Give me an undeniable understanding of how much
You care for me. In the name of Jesus I pray. Amen.

DON'T TAKE IT FOR GRANTED

Don't grieve God. Don't break his heart. His
Holy Spirit, moving and breathing in you, is the
most intimate part of your life, making you fit
for himself. Don't take such a gift for granted.
EPHESIANS 4:30 MSG

Today's verse is a call for us to cooperate with God. We are to be part of the process rather than part of the problem, always willing to follow God's leading. And in those moments when we feel weak or unqualified, it's the Holy Spirit moving in us that provides confidence. Before you were born, the Lord determined your steps. He implanted in you the skills and talents for your calling, and God used life experiences to grow and mature them. It's His Spirit that blesses you each day so you have what it takes to live a life of faith. Don't take this gift for granted.

• •

Dear God, help me be reverent toward the blessing
of Your Holy Spirit in me. Let me hear Your voice and
follow Your ways. In the name of Jesus I pray. Amen.

131

HIS PERFECTING WORK

I am confident that the Creator, who has begun such a
great work among you, will not stop in mid-design but
will keep perfecting you until the day Jesus the Anointed,
our Liberating King, returns to redeem the world.
PHILIPPIANS 1:6 VOICE

You are a work in progress. Understand that until you see Jesus face-to-face, God will continue to perfect you through life experiences. That means your faith is always under construction, and it's a blessing. So ask the Lord to give you an eternal perspective so you're able to see the struggles and battles as ways He is maturing you. Ask for wisdom so you'll know the right path to follow. Let Him fill you with strength to weather the ups and downs of life. And rather than fall into despair when those tough seasons hit, thank the Lord for every opportunity to become more like Jesus.

* *

Dear God, I'm humbled by the great lengths
You take to deepen my faith and make me more
like Your Son. Help me be moldable in Your
hands. In the name of Jesus I pray. Amen.

CERTAIN HOPE

*We have this certain hope like a strong, unbreakable
anchor holding our souls to God himself. Our
anchor of hope is fastened to the mercy seat in the
heavenly realm beyond the sacred threshold.*

HEBREWS 6:19 TPT

What a powerful image this verse offers when it says there's
certain hope that our faith anchors us to God Himself. And it's
not a small, wimpy anchor. Rather it's a strong, unbreakable
anchor. Friend, that's a beautiful promise of undeniable security.
Just think: A cruise ship's anchor can weigh up to twenty tons,
which is impressive! But then realize how small that ship is
compared to the vastness of God. While a huge storm may
loosen that ship's anchor, there is *nothing* that can separate
you from your Father in heaven. You can be full of confidence
and certainty in that promise.

• •

*Dear God, hold me tight and never let me go. No matter
the storms I face or the struggles that come my way, be
the anchor that keeps me safe and secure because of
my faith in You. In the name of Jesus I pray. Amen.*

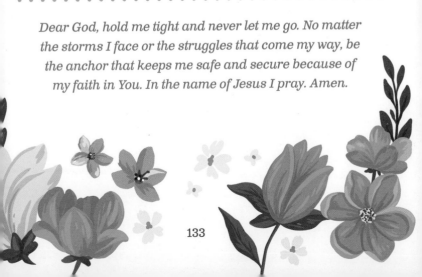

JESUS SPEAKS UP FOR YOU

Earlier there were a lot of priests, for they died and had to be replaced. But Jesus' priesthood is permanent. He's there from now to eternity to save everyone who comes to God through him, always on the job to speak up for them.

HEBREWS 7:23–25 MSG

What a blessing to realize Jesus is talking to His Father about you always. Your name is constantly on His lips. He is an informant, keeping God updated. Jesus continually advocates for you, discussing your circumstances. So in those moments when you don't have the right words and can't articulate what's weighing heavy on your heart, rest knowing Jesus is speaking up for you. And what's more, He will never stop. Yes, you are the topic of conversation in the heavenlies. How wonderful that is!

. . . .

Dear God, You really have everything covered, don't You? Even when I can't speak for myself, You have made provision. Never let me doubt how blessed I am because You love me with such magnificence. In the name of Jesus I pray. Amen.

134

IT'S ALL ABOUT JESUS

*So Jesus is the One who has enacted a new covenant with
a new relationship with God so that those who accept
the invitation will receive the eternal inheritance he has
promised to his heirs. For he died to release us from the
guilt of the violations committed under the first covenant.*

HEBREWS 9:15 TPT

Take time today to reflect on the blessing we have in Jesus
Christ. It's all about Him. He is why we can have a relationship
with God. He is why we have an eternal inheritance. He's why
we are heirs in the kingdom. It's Jesus who stepped into a
sinful world to save us. It's His blood that washed us clean and
bridged the gap sin created. Christ's death released us from
the bondage of our transgressions. Friend, Jesus is why we
can stand strong in faith. Share with Him your thankful heart.

* *

*Dear God, thank You for the blessing of Your Son.
I'm so grateful for who He is and what He has done
for me. In the name of Jesus I pray. Amen.*

135

IN ALL CIRCUMSTANCES

*I know what it means to lack, and I know what it means
to experience overwhelming abundance. For I'm trained
in the secret of overcoming all things, whether in fullness
or in hunger. And I find that the strength of Christ's
explosive power infuses me to conquer every difficulty.*

PHILIPPIANS 4:12–13 TPT

Having faith means seeing God's blessings whether in times of
plenty or scarcity. It gives us the unique ability to have joy and
peace regardless of our circumstances. The more we read God's
Word and apply it to our lives, the easier it will be to stand firm
in our faith no matter what's going on around us. Don't be shy
to ask God for help when hardship comes your way. Be quick
to lean on Him for what you need to navigate the struggles.
Because we are believers, we have access to Christ's power,
which will infuse us when we ask.

. . . .

*Dear God, help me lean on You in all circumstances. Steady
me so that whether I experience lack or abundance, my faith
is not shaken. I trust You. In the name of Jesus I pray. Amen.*

136

YOU ARE REBORN

*Celebrate with praises the God and Father of our Lord
Jesus Christ, who has shown us his extravagant mercy.
For his fountain of mercy has given us a new life—we
are reborn to experience a living, energetic hope through
the resurrection of Jesus Christ from the dead.*

1 PETER 1:3 TPT

Because of the selfless act of Jesus on the cross, we can be
reborn. His blood has the supernatural ability to cleanse
us from every sin. And it's that purification that makes you
acceptable in God's eyes. When He looks at you, friend, He sees
Jesus. Ask the Lord to give you a fresh understanding of your
salvation. Let Him remind you of the hope you have because of
the resurrection of Jesus. And choose to live a life of faith that
reflects all that Jesus has done for you. My, aren't we blessed!

* *

*Dear God, what a privilege to be reborn into the
family. I am honored to be called Your child! Thank
You for making a way for me to be with You for
eternity. In the name of Jesus I pray. Amen.*

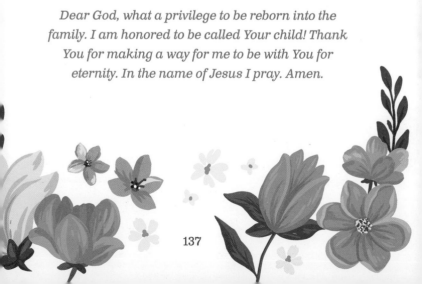

THE ENDURANCE OF GOD'S WORD

For as Isaiah said, All life is like the grass, and its glory like a flower; the grass will wither and die, and the flower falls, but the word of the Lord will endure forever. This is the word that has been preached to you.
1 PETER 1:24–25 VOICE

What a powerful reminder that everything in this world will wither and die. Nothing here is built to last. We may pursue the fountain of youth or look for ways to preserve what we have, but it will all fail in the end. So what a blessing to realize God's Word will remain alive and active forever. It's not subject to any earthly limitation. Its light won't be extinguished by anything or anyone. And it will continue to endure, just like it has for thousands of years.

. . . .

Dear God, Your Word is precious to me, and I am overwhelmed by its relevance even today. What a blessing that in a world where everything withers and dies, Your holy Word never will. In the name of Jesus I pray. Amen.

138

ONCE AND FOR ALL

Christ suffered and died for sins once and for all—the innocent for the guilty—to bring you near to God by his body being put to death and by being raised to life by the Spirit.

1 PETER 3:18 TPT

Sometimes it's hard to embrace the truth that when Jesus died for our sins, it was a once-and-done event. Many of us wear guilt like a badge. We drape ourselves in shame. And rather than accept the blessing of forgiveness when we say yes to Jesus, we choose to stay tangled in the bondage of our sin. Friend, if you're struggling to accept that your sins are fully forgiven, tell God. Let Him know the reasons why it's hard to embrace His forgiveness. Be honest about your hesitation to accept this as truth. And ask Him to bring profound revelation into full view.

• •

Dear God, help me understand the power of Jesus' sacrifice on the cross. Help me understand that every sin is forgiven. And build my confidence to embrace this amazing blessing. In the name of Jesus I pray. Amen.

GOD-GIVEN WISDOM

Blessings pour over the ones who find wisdom, for they have obtained living-understanding. As wisdom increases, a great treasure is imparted, greater than many bars of refined gold. It is a more valuable commodity than gold and gemstones, for there is nothing you desire that could compare to her.

PROVERBS 3:13–15 TPT

To have God-given wisdom is a blessing because it can't be replicated. He is the only one who can bless us with a greater understanding and a unique perspective on the things of life. It's the Lord who can open our eyes to weightier realities. He can reveal deeper truths. God can unlock insight in greater measure. And with it will come a great treasure and blessing as we pursue the Lord to help us make sense of our world.

. . . .

Dear God, nothing compares to the wisdom You provide to those who seek it. Open my eyes to see every situation with clarity, and give me creativity and strategy to move forward. I want Your wisdom to course through my veins every day. In the name of Jesus I pray. Amen.

THE BLESSING OF SURRENDER

Trust in the Lord completely, and do not rely on your own opinions. With all your heart rely on him to guide you, and he will lead you in every decision you make. Become intimate with him in whatever you do, and he will lead you wherever you go.

PROVERBS 3:5–6 TPT

There is a blessing that comes from your choice to completely surrender to God. It feels scary at times, but letting Him lead is the safest way to live because He always has our best in mind. How do we trust the Lord completely? We involve Him in our daily decisions, every one of them. We talk with God constantly, asking for guidance and direction. We wait on His leadership. We train our ears to hear His voice through His Word. Friend, ask God to bless you with the ability to surrender. It's the best decision you can make.

. . . .

Dear God, help me find the courage to take a back seat. I am giving You leadership over my life, knowing You'll guide me down the right path at the right time. In the name of Jesus I pray. Amen.

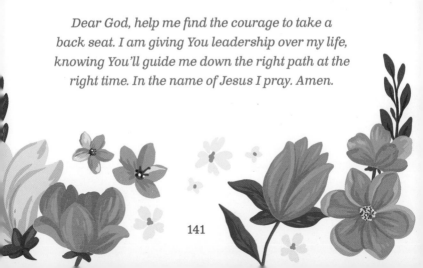

GLORIFYING GOD
WITH YOUR WEALTH

*Glorify God with all your wealth, honoring him with
your firstfruits, with every increase that comes to you.
Then every dimension of your life will overflow with
blessings from an uncontainable source of inner joy!*

PROVERBS 3:9–10 TPT

Scripture is clear that if we want an overflow of blessings and
an uncontainable source of joy, then being generous with our
finances is key. Many of us hold on to our cash because it makes
us feel safe and secure. We're conditioned to save for a rainy
day. While we give a little here or there, chances are we've been
raised to cling to our cash or to prioritize spending it on our
hearts' desire. And we wonder why we feel blah. Why not give
today's verses a try? What have you got to lose?

* *

*Dear God, forgive me for not taking every opportunity
to glorify You with my wealth. Honestly, it scares me
to let go of my money. Bless me with a sense of peace
and a greater measure of faith to follow this command
with expectation. In the name of Jesus I pray. Amen.*

THE BLESSING OF WISDOM AND PURPOSE

My child, never drift off course from these two goals for your life: to walk in wisdom and to discover your purpose. Don't ever forget how they empower you. For they strengthen you inside and out and inspire you to do what's right; you will be energized and refreshed by the healing they bring.

PROVERBS 3:21–22 TPT

If you want to be blessed from the inside out, able to discern right from wrong with clarity, then set two things at the top of your priority list. First, ask God for wisdom for the road ahead. Second, ask Him to reveal your purpose. Together, this power-packed duo will empower you to live a blessed life of faith! Wisdom and purpose will help direct your decisions so God will be glorified. And they'll bring healing as you focus on Him, strengthening your resolve to do the right thing.

. . . .

Dear God, bless me through Your wisdom and revelation of my purpose. Help me keep both at the helm so they're what guide me, keeping my faith on track. In the name of Jesus I pray. Amen.

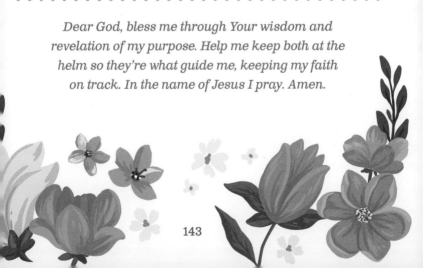

THE REWARD FOR KINDNESS

Whoever cares for the poor makes a loan to the Eternal;
such kindness will be repaid in full and with interest.
PROVERBS 19:17 VOICE

Let's not choose to be kind just because we know there's a blessing involved. But realizing that our kindness delights God's heart must be a factor. When we become a follower of Jesus, it will change us. Our hearts will be tendered. We'll be filled with compassion for the lost and broken. And we'll want to make a difference in the world. So when we care for the poor, it should be a result of our faith. What's so beautiful is God's promise to bless our obedience when we do. It's like positive reinforcement for stepping out of our comfort zone and being His hands and feet. What a blessing to know our kindness will be acknowledged and rewarded by God!

* *

Dear God, what a great reminder of the value
You put on kindness and generosity. Let me be an
extension of Your love to a broken and hurting
world. In the name of Jesus I pray. Amen.

144

EVERY PROMISE FULFILLED

*So He gave them rest from war on every side as He
had sworn to their ancestors; none of their enemies
still stood against them, for the Eternal had delivered
them all into their hands. Not a single one of all the
good promises that He had made to the house of
Israel went unfulfilled; all of them came to pass.*

JOSHUA 21:44–45 VOICE

When God makes a promise, it is unbreakable. Friend, you
can have full faith that it will come to pass at the right time.
God doesn't change His mind, which should give you great
confidence to trust His Word as truth. Tell God where you're
struggling today. Let Him know what is weighing heavy on
your heart. And open your eyes and ears for the promises He
has in store for you. Yes, God will bless you with His goodness
as He keeps His Word.

. . . .

*Dear God, increase my faith so I can embrace
the truth of Your trustworthiness. In a world of
broken promises, fill my heart with gratitude
that You stand alone in unshakable integrity.
In the name of Jesus I pray. Amen.*

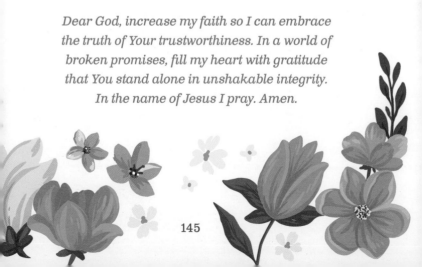

THANKING GOD
FOR COMMUNITY

So let's do it—full of belief, confident that we're presentable inside and out. Let's keep a firm grip on the promises that keep us going. He always keeps his word. Let's see how inventive we can be in encouraging love and helping out, not avoiding worshiping together as some do but spurring each other on, especially as we see the big Day approaching.
HEBREWS 10:22–25 MSG

Community is such a powerful tool for encouragement. No wonder God calls our attention to it countless times in His Word. Think of the wonderful family and friends who surround you. They are most certainly not perfect, but they bless you in profound ways. They're the ones who steady you if you're struggling in your marriage or parenting. They're the ones who hold your hand as the doctor unpacks your treatment plan. They're the ones who step up to meet your basic needs when you can't. And even though community can be super messy at times, thank God for the blessings it brings into your life.

. . . .

Dear God, I appreciate the reminder of the value community provides. Thank You! In the name of Jesus I pray. Amen.

146

A GUIDING STAR

We are cracked and chipped from our afflictions
on all sides, but we are not crushed by them. We are
bewildered at times, but we do not give in to despair.
We are persecuted, but we have not been abandoned.
We have been knocked down, but we are not destroyed.
2 CORINTHIANS 4:8–9 VOICE

Friend, let today's scripture wash over you like a tidal wave of blessings. Let this be what encourages you to stand strong as you face Goliaths. Hold on to the truths in this passage when you're struggling to hold on a second longer. It's because of your faith that you can claim this passage as your guiding star. God never promised an easy life, but He did send His Son to overcome the world. So when you feel overwhelmed, you will not be crushed. You won't give in to despair, because you've not been abandoned. And no matter what, you will not be destroyed. Be blessed!

• •

Dear God, thank You for the reminder of the life
I have in You! In the name of Jesus I pray. Amen.

SHORT-LIVED INCONVENIENCES

So we have no reason to despair. Despite the fact that our outer humanity is falling apart and decaying, our inner humanity is breathing in new life every day. You see, the short-lived pains of this life are creating for us an eternal glory that does not compare to anything we know here.

2 CORINTHIANS 4:16–17 VOICE

What a relief to know that while our bodies may be suffering the effects of living in a sinful world, our spirits inside can be full of vigor and refreshment! The reality is that we will suffer hardship as long as we're breathing on planet Earth. Relationships will fall apart. Finances will fail. We'll face a myriad of health challenges. And yes, we will also battle with insecurity and shame and fear. But these are short-lived inconveniences that pale in comparison to the blessings we'll experience in heaven!

. . . .

Dear God, what a blessing to realize that while my body and mind may be subject to the negative effects of this world, my spirit can be soaring at the same time. In the name of Jesus I pray. Amen.

148

INVESTING IN ETERNITY

*There's far more here than meets the eye. The things
we see now are here today, gone tomorrow. But
the things we can't see now will last forever.*

2 CORINTHIANS 4:18 MSG

Let's remember that everything we can see with our eyes will one day be gone. We can't take anything we store up here into eternity. So then why do we spend so much time collecting earthly treasure? Why do our efforts fall there, especially considering the blessings that await us for storing up treasures in heaven instead? Today, meditate on the truth that every time you choose to obey God's commands there's a deposit made in the heavenlies. Set your gaze on living and loving in the ways the Lord has commanded.

. . . .

*Dear God, what a great reminder to invest in the
things of heaven rather than focus my time and
treasure on the things of this world. Help me see
the difference. And give me the wisdom to invest
well in eternity. In the name of Jesus I pray. Amen.*

JESUS IS THE "YES"

*For all of God's promises find their "yes" of
fulfillment in him. And as his "yes" and our
"amen" ascend to God, we bring him glory!*
2 CORINTHIANS 1:20 TPT

Jesus is the "yes" answer to all God's promises. He is the One
who punctuates the end of the sentence. Jesus dots the *i*'s and
crosses the *t*'s. He is able to bring everything into full bloom.
That's exactly why we say a hearty *amen* through His name,
bringing glory to God. Whenever you submit a request through
prayer, pray in the name of Jesus. Every time you ask for help
or healing or wisdom, end your ask with His name. Jesus is
where the power in your prayer comes from. Jesus opens every
door to His Father.

· ·

*Dear God, once again I share my gratitude for Your
Son, Jesus. Thank You for giving us access to Yourself
and every blessing through Him. There is power in
the name of Jesus! In His holy name I pray. Amen.*

EMBRACING COMMUNITY

Bless your enemies; no cursing under your breath.
Laugh with your happy friends when they're
happy; share tears when they're down. Get along
with each other; don't be stuck-up. Make friends
with nobodies; don't be the great somebody.
ROMANS 12:14–16 MSG

God is asking us to embrace community. He is encouraging us
to love one another. Why might that be? Maybe He knows the
power of unity. Maybe it's because He understands the beauty
of living in peace with one another. Or maybe it's because
God knows we need kindness and generosity in this world.
Regardless, it's clear in His Word that He blesses those who obey
Him. Oh yes, the Lord is committed to rewarding the faithful.
So be intentional to live in such a way that others benefit from
your friendship. It will delight God's heart!

• •

Dear God, remind me of the value placed on obeying Your
Word. Let me embrace the call to love others. I want to be a
blessing, especially in these crazy times. Everyone is blessed
by an encourager. In the name of Jesus I pray. Amen.

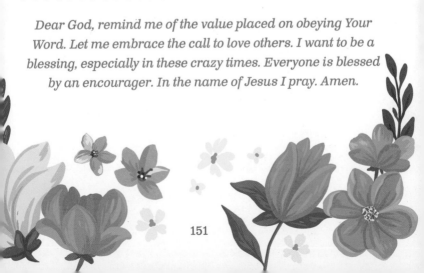

151

STOP IMITATING

Stop imitating the ideals and opinions of the culture around you, but be inwardly transformed by the Holy Spirit through a total reformation of how you think. This will empower you to discern God's will as you live a beautiful life, satisfying and perfect in his eyes.

ROMANS 12:2 TPT

This verse is a challenge to take your eyes off what the world promises and refocus your heart on God. We can easily get caught up in what's trending, investing our hearts in the here and now. But when you desire to follow God and His commands, the Holy Spirit will transform you. He'll empower you. And you'll find the strength to think on the things of God rather than run on the treadmill of perfection, fueled by the ideas and opinions of the world. You'll be blessed as you live a beautiful life honoring your Father in heaven.

• •

Dear God, I don't want to imitate the world, because there's nothing here for me. Help me surrender my will and experience the powerful transformation through Your Holy Spirit. In the name of Jesus I pray. Amen.

GRACE-GIFTS

*If you have the grace-gift of encouragement, then use it
often to encourage others. If you have the grace-gift of
giving to meet the needs of others, then may you prosper
in your generosity without any fanfare. If you have the
gift of leadership, be passionate about your leadership.
And if you have the gift of showing compassion, then
flourish in your cheerful display of compassion.*

ROMANS 12:8 TPT

We all have grace-gifts from the Lord. When He created us,
God decided on the gifts we would bring to the body of Christ.
Together, we make a beautiful and well-rounded community
of believers. Think of your friends and the different ways they
support others. Some are full of compassion; some are good at
initiating action. Some may have vision and others are prayer
warriors. Friend, use your gift well.

• •

*Dear God, open my eyes to see the grace-gift You have
deposited in me. Help me recognize opportunities to
bless others with it. In the name of Jesus I pray. Amen.*

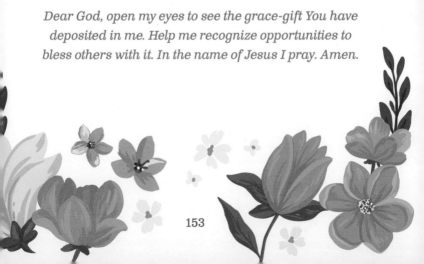

EXCITEMENT TO SHARE

Be enthusiastic to serve the Lord, keeping your passion
toward him boiling hot! Radiate with the glow of the
Holy Spirit and let him fill you with excitement as
you serve him. Let this hope burst forth within you,
releasing a continual joy. Don't give up in a time
of trouble, but commune with God at all times.
ROMANS 12:11–12 TPT

It's a privilege and a blessing to serve God with our lives. As a matter of fact, our hearts' desire should be for our words and actions to point to God in heaven. But sometimes we struggle, thinking our need to promote the Lord is a chore. We view it as an annoyance or time drain. But His Word says to be enthusiastic about serving. It says to radiate with the Spirit's glow! Is that a challenge for you? Ask God to fill you with excitement as you serve. Let's be women who joyfully share our faith with others.

· ·

Dear God, let me share You with passion and purpose
every chance I get. In the name of Jesus I pray. Amen.

154

VENGEANCE IS NOT OURS

Beloved, don't be obsessed with taking revenge, but leave that to God's righteous justice. For the Scriptures say: "Vengeance is mine, and I will repay," says the Lord. And: If your enemy is hungry, buy him lunch! Win him over with kindness. For your surprising generosity will awaken his conscience, and God will reward you with favor. Never let evil defeat you, but defeat evil with good.

ROMANS 12:19–21 TPT

It's difficult to show kindness to your enemy. Many struggle to be generous with the ones who've hurt us the most. But God commands us to trust Him to make right what has gone very wrong. He wants vengeance to be His alone. And when we trust Him in this, it frees us up to be compassionate and caring. With His help, we can live in victory rather than defeat. Yes, we can bless instead of curse.

. . . .

Dear God, I confess this is hard. I want to hurt those who hurt me. So fill my heart with peace in knowing You will take care of justice, perfectly. In the name of Jesus I pray. Amen.

IT BLESSES GOD

*"Then those 'sheep' are going to say, 'Master, what are
you talking about? When did we ever see you hungry
and feed you, thirsty and give you a drink? And when
did we ever see you sick or in prison and come to you?'
Then the King will say, 'I'm telling the solemn truth:
Whenever you did one of these things to someone
overlooked or ignored, that was me—you did it to me.'"*
MATTHEW 25:37–40 MSG

Make no mistake, God notices when we are kind and generous
to others. He sees it every time we're His hands and feet. It's
so important that God takes it personally. He tells us that in
each situation where we show compassion to someone, it's
like showing compassion to Him. When we use our time and
treasure to bless others, it blesses Him. And what a gift to us—
knowing we were able to delight the heart of God.

. . . .

*Dear God, I love knowing that when I'm kind and
generous to someone here, that kindness and
generosity transfers to You in heaven. Let that be
my motivation. In the name of Jesus I pray. Amen.*

BLESSED BY PERSISTENCE

"Ask, and the gift is yours. Seek, and you'll discover. Knock, and the door will be opened for you. For every persistent one will get what he asks for. Every persistent seeker will discover what he longs for. And everyone who knocks persistently will one day find an open door."

MATTHEW 7:7–8 TPT

There is a reward to be given for your persistence in faith. God is ready to honor those who seek Him with all their heart. Every time we go to the Lord, He hears our cry and blesses us with His heavenly response. God doesn't try to hide from us. He doesn't make it difficult to be found. And scripture tells us that when we are unrelenting and tenacious in finding our answers in Him, we will be blessed by His presence.

. . . .

Dear God, give me unshakable faith to wait on You. Give me endurance as I wait for the right doors to open at the right time. And let me find all my answers in You. In the name of Jesus I pray. Amen.

YOU HAVE THE BEST PARENT

"If you, imperfect as you are, know how to lovingly take care of your children and give them what's best, how much more ready is your heavenly Father to give wonderful gifts to those who ask him?"

MATTHEW 7:11 TPT

We are never too old to be parented, especially when that parent is our Father in heaven. He knows exactly what we need to take the next step forward. He knows everything that tangles us in fear and insecurity. He understands what motivates us. God sees the answer to every struggle we face. He knows the exact time we need Him to intervene and when we need to stand and fight in His strength. There is no one who comes close to loving us with the steadfast love of God. Be blessed in knowing you have the best parent with you always.

* *

Dear God, what a relief to know You will take care of me always. It's blessed assurance, and I'm so grateful! In the name of Jesus I pray. Amen.

DO UNTO OTHERS

This is what our Scriptures come to teach:
in everything, in every circumstance, do to
others as you would have them do to you.
MATTHEW 7:12 VOICE

This simple concept is so hard to walk out at times. Why? Because we don't always immediately see the fruit. We can choose to forgive, but we may not be forgiven by others quickly. We can show kindness and be met with mean-spiritedness in return. And we may give generously to those who need it yet find no generosity in our time of need. Regardless, God still commands us to treat others as we want and hope to be treated. It may never be reciprocated on earth, but make no mistake: God sees your heart and effort. He will bless you as you pursue righteous living. Your reward may come only from the Father, and that is enough.

• •

Dear God, help me treat others in the ways I
hope to be treated. And if they do not respond in
the same manner, remind me of Your blessings.
In the name of Jesus I pray. Amen.

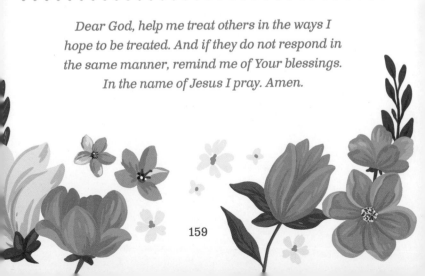

159

A FIRM FOUNDATION

Those people who are listening to Me, those people who hear what I say and live according to My teachings—you are like a wise man who built his house on a rock, on a firm foundation. When storms hit, rain pounded down and waters rose, levies broke and winds beat all the walls of that house. But the house did not fall because it was built upon rock.

MATTHEW 7:24–25 VOICE

Be blessed and encouraged by today's scripture! Let it affirm your daily choice to live a life full of faith—not perfectly, but purposefully. Every time you hear God and follow His leading, He calls you wise. In every situation where you follow His holy Word, your obedience will be rewarded. The truth is life comes at us fast sometimes. It hits hard. It knocks us to our knees and breaks our hearts. But when we trust God, our foundation is firm. We may be shaken, but we will not crumble. God blesses the ones who build their lives in Him.

* *

*Dear God, let my life be built on You alone.
In the name of Jesus I pray. Amen.*

BEFORE AND BEHIND

The Eternal has flexed His muscles, bared His holy arm for the world to see His power; every nation, every person, every place on earth will witness the victory of our God. . . . Go in confidence and grace— no rushing, no frantic escape. There's no need to be anxious—the Eternal One goes before and behind you. The God of Israel paves the way with assurance and strength. He watches your back.

ISAIAH 52:10, 12 VOICE

Imagine facing dire circumstances without fear or anxiety. Think of what a gift it would be to stand strong in your troubles without frantically looking for a way out. What if you had courage and confidence to believe God was already working through the situations that bring you grief? There's no one stronger than the Lord, so let Him be who strengthens you for every battle. If scripture says He has gone before and stands behind you, then it's true and you can believe it by faith. Friend, you're blessed with a mighty God who never backs down!

. . . .

*Dear God, You are all I need.
In the name of Jesus I pray. Amen.*

SOUL CELEBRATION

*With my whole heart, with my whole life, and with my
innermost being, I bow in wonder and love before you, the
holy God! Yahweh, you are my soul's celebration. How could
I ever forget the miracles of kindness you've done for me?*

PSALM 103:1–2 TPT

When we purpose to fully understand—as much as we humanly
can—the goodness of God, we'll be overwhelmed. Every moment
of every day the Lord has been with you. He's never left you to
suffer alone. He's never abandoned you for another. He's never
rejected you in times of need. Once these truths sink deep into
the marrow of your bones, you'll be filled with wonder and awe.
In that moment, you will recognize the sacred ground you stand
on. Ask God to bless you with this depth of understanding so
your soul celebrates in reverence.

. . . .

*Dear God, I don't have the right words to adequately
express my gratitude for who You are and how
You love me. Look into my heart and know my
appreciation. In the name of Jesus I pray. Amen.*

162

RENEWED WITH TRUTH

*You kissed my heart with forgiveness, in spite of all
I've done. You've healed me inside and out from every
disease. You've rescued me from hell and saved my life.
You've crowned me with love and mercy. You satisfy my
every desire with good things. You've supercharged my
life so that I soar again like a flying eagle in the sky!*

PSALM 103:3–5 TPT

These verses are packed full of blessings. In them, we learn that
God forgives us. He has healed us. He's rescued and saved in His
sovereignty. We are crowned with His love. Every desire we have
will be satisfied in Him. And our lives have been supernaturally
supercharged, so we are able to experience the power of Jesus'
freedom. In those moments when you feel unloved or unblessed,
revisit this passage of scripture. Let it renew your heart and
mind to know the truth of how much God loves you.

· ·

*Dear God, You have done so much for me. Forgive
me for not seeing the depth of Your goodness.
I see it now! In the name of Jesus I pray. Amen.*

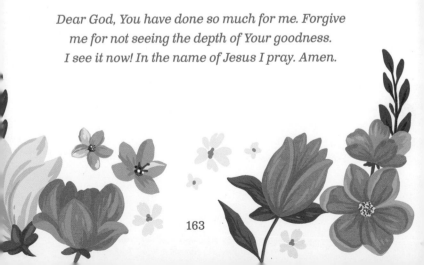

163

GOD ISN'T LOOKING FOR FAULTS

*Lord, you're so kind and tenderhearted and so
patient with people who fail you! Your love is like a
flooding river overflowing its banks with kindness.
You don't look at us only to find our faults, just
so that you can hold a grudge against us.*

PSALM 103:8–9 TPT

Isn't it wonderful to read how kind and tenderhearted our Father in heaven is toward us? And knowing His love has nothing to do with us being flawless makes it even sweeter. Friend, we will fail Him. We will disobey His commands, which are very clear. We will let Him down both accidentally and willfully at times. We will direct our anger toward Him when He isn't the rightful target. We will allow Him to fall farther down our list of importance, often without realizing it. But God doesn't look at us to find fault. He doesn't hold grudges. Instead, His heart overflows with loving-kindness toward us. Receive that as a beautiful blessing today.

• •

*Dear God, thank You for being You.
In the name of Jesus I pray. Amen.*

HIGHER AND GREATER

*Higher than the highest heavens—that's how high
your tender mercy extends! Greater than the grandeur of
heaven above is the greatness of your loyal love, towering
over all who fear you and bow down before you!*

PSALM 103:11 TPT

Talk about loving big! It's overwhelming to try to understand the measurements of God's love. Our world is full of restrictions. As humans, we face the reality of our own limits every day. We can only forgive so much. We only have the ability to love so deep. We are only able to bless others with our time and treasure in rations. Yes, we are used to boundaries and borders. So the truth that God's mercy and love are inexhaustible takes a moment to settle in. Ask Him to help you realize the blessings His infinite compassion offers.

· ·

*Dear God, I love the fact that Your compassion for
me is immeasurable. I love that it has no limits. That
frees me up to live my imperfect life in pursuit of
righteousness. In the name of Jesus I pray. Amen.*

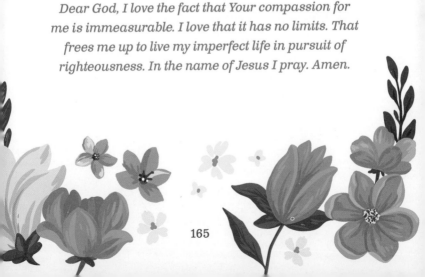

GOD KNOWS YOU INSIDE AND OUT

The same way a loving father feels toward his children—that's but a sample of your tender feelings toward us, your beloved children, who live in awe of you. You know all about us, inside and out. You are mindful that we're made from dust.

PSALM 103:13–14 TPT

Some might feel exposed or embarrassed to learn that God knows them inside and out. There may be guilt or shame involved. It may trigger deep insecurities. But the reality is that being known in this way by a trustworthy God is absolutely beautiful. We don't have to be a certain way to receive His love. There's no expectation of perfection. He delights in us simply because we are His. Today, thank Him for caring so deeply and knowing you so fully. Let that bless your weary heart in fresh ways.

. . . .

Dear God, I'm blessed in the revelation that You want to know me. So often I feel unseen and unvalued, but I realize now, that is simply not true. In the name of Jesus I pray. Amen.

ENDLESS LOVE

But Lord, your endless love stretches from one eternity
to the other, unbroken and unrelenting toward those
who fear you and those who bow facedown in awe
before you. Your faithfulness to keep every gracious
promise you've made passes from parents, to children,
to grandchildren, and beyond. You are faithful to all
those who follow your ways and keep your word.
PSALM 103:17–18 TPT

The truth is that God is faithful to everyone who follows His ways and holds steady to His Word. Too often, we underestimate the powerful blessings that come from obedience. We struggle to see the weightiness of His unwavering promises. We don't fully grasp the height, width, and depth of His steadfast love. So friend, let today's passage of scripture be an eye-opener. God's love is endless. It can't be broken. It can't be tainted. And His blessings can span generations.

Dear God, thank You for loving me completely and
fully. Thank You for recognizing my obedience
through Your blessings. Help me live faithfully.
In the name of Jesus I pray. Amen.

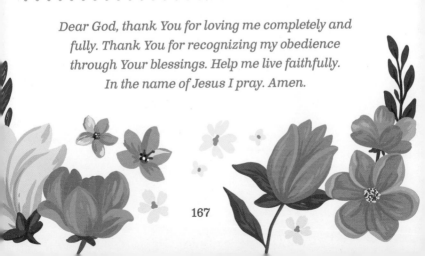

SEEING GOD'S BLESSINGS

Bless and praise the Lord, you mighty warriors,
ministers who serve him well and fulfill his desires.
I will bless and praise the Lord with my whole heart!
Let all his works throughout the earth, wherever his
dominion stretches—let everything bless the Lord!
PSALM 103:21–22 TPT

This is a challenge to see God's goodness in our lives. It's a call to praise Him for the ways He's intersected our circumstances. It takes intentionality on our part to recognize God's hand moving in our situations. Take some time today to remember where you've seen the Lord bless your life or the lives of those you love. Talk to Him about what His intervention has meant. Thank Him for perfect timing and perfect ways. Friend, what would we do without God?

* *

Dear God, my eyes are open, and I see Your power
throughout my life. I'm humbled by the ways You love me.
I'm grateful for the ways You've blessed me. Let my life
bless You back! In the name of Jesus I pray. Amen.

THE JUDGMENT SEAT

How blessed the man you train, GOD, the woman you instruct in your Word, providing a circle of quiet within the clamor of evil, while a jail is being built for the wicked. GOD will never walk away from his people, never desert his precious people. Rest assured that justice is on its way and every good heart put right.

PSALM 94:12–15 MSG

It's a blessing to know justice is on its way. So often, we want to take it into our own hands and repay evil for evil. We want to hurt the ones who have hurt us the most. We want to pay back suffering for suffering to even the score. And many of us spend way too much time plotting and scheming because it makes us feel better, if only for a moment. But it's God who will sit in the judgment seat. He is the one who will make right all of the wrongs. You can trust Him with your heart.

• •

Dear God, build my confidence that You will bring to justice the ones who deserve it. In the name of Jesus I pray. Amen.

169

ALWAYS FOR YOU AND WITH YOU

Who stood up for me against the wicked? Who took my side against evil workers? If GOD hadn't been there for me, I never would have made it. The minute I said, "I'm slipping, I'm falling," your love, GOD, took hold and held me fast. When I was upset and beside myself, you calmed me down and cheered me up.

PSALM 94:16–19 MSG

In those moments when you feel all alone, wondering if anyone is going to come to your aid, remember that God is always for you and with you. You may feel completely abandoned and fully rejected, but that's not the reality of your situation. The truth is anytime you cry out for God's help, He is there. Every time you need someone to hold you steady and calm your anxious heart, the Lord is willing and able. Friend, be blessed in knowing God will help you walk through any struggle that comes your way.

* *

Dear God, thank You for catching me every time I begin to slip and fall. You are my rescuer. In the name of Jesus I pray. Amen.

LET GOD BE YOUR HIDEOUT

*Can Misrule have anything in common with you? Can
Troublemaker pretend to be on your side? They ganged up
on good people, plotted behind the backs of the innocent. But
GOD became my hideout, God was my high mountain retreat,
then boomeranged their evil back on them: for their evil ways
he wiped them out, our GOD cleaned them out for good.*

PSALM 94:20–23 MSG

Sometimes we need a hideaway from the difficulties and pain
of this world. We need somewhere to tuck away from our
worries and fears. And these are the times we're desperate
for God to fight on our behalf and bring resolution to the chaos
surrounding us. If He isn't already, make the Lord your place
of safety. Let Him be the one who blesses you with peace and
comfort. Trust Him with your weary heart. God loves you and
will care for you!

. . . .

*Dear God, let me hide my face in Your chest as I wait
for You to bring restoration. I simply cannot battle
this alone. In the name of Jesus I pray. Amen.*

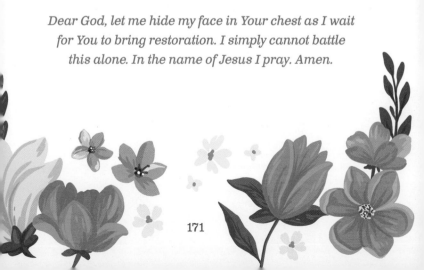

171

THE ABILITY TO ABIDE

*He will make you the head, not the tail; you'll always be
on top and never on the bottom—if you'll just listen to the
commands I'm giving you today from the Eternal your
God, and obey them carefully. All these blessings will
be yours if you don't deviate at all, neither to the right
nor to the left, from any of the things I'm commanding
you today, if you don't go and worship other gods!*
DEUTERONOMY 28:13–14 VOICE

There's no wiggle room when God gives a command. You may
try to find some or look for ways to justify deviating from His
will. In your rebellious spirit, you might see how far you can
push things. But when the Lord gives a command and you
follow it, a blessing is certain to bloom. Because we often need
His strength to walk this out, be quick to ask the Lord for the
ability to abide.

. . . .

*Dear God, help me obey Your will for my life.
And let me thrive in the blessings that come
from it. In the name of Jesus I pray. Amen.*

UNCHANGING LOVE FOR YOU

GOD, your God, refused to listen to Balaam but turned the curse into a blessing—how GOD, your God, loves you! Don't even try to get along with them or do anything for them, ever.

DEUTERONOMY 23:5–6 MSG

No one can sway the heart of God when it comes to you. No one can change His mind about your magnificence. God sees the challenges you face as well as the areas of celebration, and He loves you unwaveringly. People may curse you, may speak terrible things about who you are or what you've done, and may even ask God to punish you, but He will never waver in His love. Be blessed in knowing the Lord can love you no more or no less than He does in this very moment. His heart for you is always good, and nothing will ever change that.

• •

Dear God, knowing how You feel about me allows me to exhale with relief. Thank You that nothing anyone says about me will ever persuade You to walk away. In the name of Jesus I pray. Amen.

173

GOD'S DIVINE POWER

His divine power has given us everything we need to experience life and to reflect God's true nature through the knowledge of the One who called us by His glory and virtue. Through these things, we have received God's great and valuable promises, so we might escape the corruption of worldly desires and share in the divine nature.

2 PETER 1:3–4 VOICE

Through God's power, we're able to find refuge from the depravity and immorality running rampant in this world. We may be in the world, but we're not of it. Our faith in Jesus allows us to experience great and valuable promises that come from believing. Don't try to handle things on your own. Don't let your pride keep you from opening your heart to God. He called us to be His, blessing us with power and might and wisdom. We don't have to live in bondage. Even while still on earth, we can experience His divine nature through faith.

. . . .

Dear God, what a beautiful blessing to experience Your divine power in the here and now. In the name of Jesus I pray. Amen.

A BEAUTIFUL HARVEST

But the wisdom from above is always pure, filled with peace, considerate and teachable. It is filled with love and never displays prejudice or hypocrisy in any form and it always bears the beautiful harvest of righteousness! Good seeds of wisdom's fruit will be planted with peaceful acts by those who cherish making peace.

JAMES 3:17–18 TPT

Simply put, you can trust God's wisdom. When you read passages in the Bible, you can believe them. Everything in God's Word is true and perfect instruction for how to live a life of righteousness. It's our handbook to navigate this life and a beautiful challenge to have faith in God. From it, let the seeds of His wisdom be planted and brought into full fruition through the Holy Spirit. What a beautiful harvest of blessings to come!

• •

Dear God, I'm so grateful You fill in the gaps and make up the differences when it comes to my human limitations. Help me be quick to ask for Your wisdom so I can live with passion and purpose, always bringing glory to Your name. In the name of Jesus I pray. Amen.

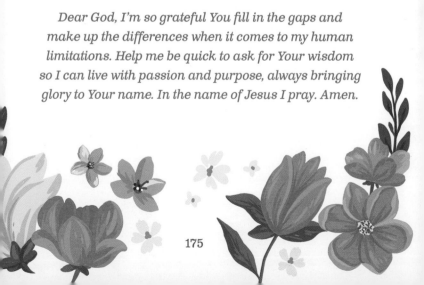

PERMISSION TO WALK AWAY

Walk away from the evil things in the world—just leave them behind, and do what is right, and always seek peace and pursue it. For the Lord watches over the righteous, and His ears are attuned to their prayers. But His face is set against His enemies; He will punish evildoers.

1 PETER 3:11–12 VOICE

For Pete's sake, get out of there! When a trial or temptation is staring you down, turn around and walk away. Don't allow anything or anyone to persuade you to compromise your beliefs and what you know is right. Don't dance around the fires of faithlessness, because you will be burned. Instead, ask God to strengthen your resolve to live in righteousness before your feet hit the floor in the morning. Let Him bless and empower you to make godly choices every day.

. . . .

Dear God, give me the courage to walk away from anything that pulls me from You. I simply can't fathom being out of Your will. Help me stand strong as I pursue righteous living. In the name of Jesus I pray. Amen.

USING OUR WORDS CAREFULLY

*We use our tongue to praise God our Father and
then turn around and curse a person who was made
in his very image! Out of the same mouth we pour
out words of praise one minute and curses the next.
My brothers and sisters, this should never be!*

JAMES 3:9–10 TPT

Ouch, right? The Bible is sharper than any double-edged sword, that's for sure! And as we've talked about before, we know God's Word is crystal clear when it says He blesses obedient living. Countless times we learn throughout the scriptures that when we choose to do what God has asked and live in the ways He's commanded, there are beautiful and meaningful blessings that come our way. Today's scripture is no exception. Let's choose to be women who speak with kindness and generosity, not allowing our words to tear anyone down. It will not go unnoticed by God.

. . . .

*Dear God, I confess I've cursed and blessed with my tongue.
Help me be mindful of the words I speak, and let them
glorify Your name. In the name of Jesus I pray. Amen.*

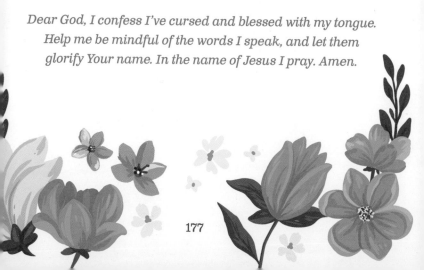

BE READY TO TELL

But give reverent honor in your hearts to the Anointed One and treat him as the holy Master of your lives. And if anyone asks about the hope living within you, always be ready to explain your faith with gentleness and respect. Maintain a clean conscience, so that those who slander you for living a pure life in Christ will have to lie about you and will be ashamed because of their slander.

1 PETER 3:15–16 TPT

Be ready to tell people why you're blessed. When good things happen, don't shy away from sharing how God's goodness intersected heartbreaking situations. Let others see how His kindness has brought relief. Be quick to share the hope you have because of the Lord. And every chance you get to encourage others to wait on His help, do it. Speak your testimony with passion and purpose. Never stop talking about the blessings you've experienced because of your faith in our Father in heaven. Friend, let others know!

. . . .

Dear God, I will tell about Your goodness every chance I get! In the name of Jesus I pray. Amen.

THE ONLY REASON
TO BOAST OR BRAG

*If you consider yourself to be wise and one who
understands the ways of God, advertise it with a
beautiful, fruitful life guided by wisdom's gentleness.
Never brag or boast about what you've done and you'll
prove that you're truly wise. But if there is bitter jealousy
or competition hiding in your heart, then don't deny it and
try to compensate for it by boasting and being phony.*
JAMES 3:13–14 TPT

The truth is this life is not about you. You may be amazing at lots
of things, but singing your own praises shows little spiritual
maturity. In the same vein, feeling jealousy to the point of
overcompensating only proves you're still living for yourself.
But friend, beautiful blessings will come when you are more
interested in advertising our amazing God than anything else.
Let His goodness be the only reason you boast or brag.

• •

*Dear God, thank You for the reminder that it's not about me.
Let everything I do and everything I say confirm the truth
that it's all about You. In the name of Jesus I pray. Amen.*

179

THE CALL TO BE KIND
AND GENEROUS

*We will show mercy to the poor and not miss an
opportunity to do acts of kindness for others, for
these are the true sacrifices that delight God's heart.*

HEBREWS 13:16 TPT

Sometimes we close off our hearts to others. Maybe it's because
we've been hurt too many times before. Maybe it's because
we're on a selfish streak. Maybe it's because we're scared to
put ourselves out there again. Regardless, God is asking each
of us to be kind and generous with our time and treasure. We're
to be sacrificial instead of self-serving. And if He's asking us to
be that for others, be blessed knowing He's asking others to be
that for us as well. As believers, our lives should be focused on
doing God's work so His name is glorified.

. . . .

*Dear God, I don't want to waste my life by focusing
on my needs. I don't want to live selfishly. Create
in my heart a desire to be kind and generous
in every way, knowing blessings will come
from it. In the name of Jesus I pray. Amen.*

CREATED FOR COMMUNITY

*Stay on good terms with each other, held together by love.
Be ready with a meal or a bed when it's needed. Why, some
have extended hospitality to angels without ever knowing it!*
HEBREWS 13:1–2 MSG

Friend, God created you for community. His plan was for us
to love one another deeply, to be ready and willing to help out
in times of need. We are the ones to bring compassion to the
broken. Together, we are a force for good to those who need
hope. We are the Lord's hands and feet, sharing His goodness
throughout our communities, our nation, and the world. As
the faithful, it's our privilege and burden to love in tangible
ways. And while we are busy doing our Father's work serving
others, we're often the ones blessed the most. We can feel God's
delight deep in our spirits.

. . . .

*Dear God, I am thankful for the opportunity to love Your
people. Thank You for community. Let me embrace
it every day. In the name of Jesus I pray. Amen.*

THE EMPTINESS INSIDE

Don't be obsessed with getting more material things.
Be relaxed with what you have. Since God assured us,
"I'll never let you down, never walk off and leave you,"
we can boldly quote, God is there, ready to help; I'm
fearless no matter what. Who or what can get to me?
HEBREWS 13:5–6 MSG

When you truly realize the blessing of God's presence and promises in your life, it will cure you of wanting more of what this world has to offer. He will be the one to fill that emptiness inside. God will meet every need. He will be the one to settle your anxious heart in healthy ways. For many of us, shopping is a coping mechanism. Every purchase brings momentary happiness. But God is always there, ready to offer lasting hope through faith. And that's the kind of blessing that will endure.

* *

Dear God, help my heart be content so I'm not always
striving for more. I know You are more than enough and
everything I need! In the name of Jesus I pray. Amen.

FAITH OPENS YOUR HEART

Faith opened Noah's heart to receive revelation and warnings from God about what was coming, even things that had never been seen. But he stepped out in reverent obedience to God and built an ark that would save him and his family. By his faith the world was condemned, but Noah received God's gift of righteousness that comes by believing.

HEBREWS 11:7 TPT

Just as faith opened Noah's heart to hear God, your time spent with Him will do the same. When you invest in studying the Bible and praying, it sharpens your spirit to hear what the Lord has to say. It makes you more in tune with His voice that offers guidance and wisdom every day. There's a beautiful blessing that comes from intimate fellowship with God because it creates an expectancy that He will speak to you. Your part is to believe.

• •

Dear God, give me the eyes to see Your hand and the ears to hear Your voice in my life. In the name of Jesus I pray. Amen.

183

A FLOODGATE OF BLESSINGS

Faith opened the way for the Hebrews to cross the Red
Sea as if on dry land, but when the Egyptians tried
to cross they were swallowed up and drowned!
HEBREWS 11:29 TPT

When we activate our faith in God, it sets the stage for Him to show off His magnificent power! Imagine the fear the Israelites felt with the sea in front of them and the Egyptian army behind them. They desperately prayed for a way out. They collectively prayed for God to save them. They cried out for the Lord to show up in a big way. And with all eyes focused, God parted the sea. God's people walked through on dry ground—a supernatural miracle! Friend, you can trust God with the circumstances weighing you down right now. You can cling to Him for a rescue. Your faith will open a floodgate of blessings, signs, and wonders.

• •

Dear God, thank You that You're still a God of miracles.
Thank You that You're still in the business of blessing
those who love You. In the name of Jesus I pray. Amen.

GOD'S EMPOWERING PRESENCE

Yet we don't see ourselves as capable enough to do anything in our own strength, for our true competence flows from God's empowering presence. He alone makes us adequate ministers who are focused on an entirely new covenant. Our ministry is not based on the letter of the law but through the power of the Spirit. The letter of the law kills, but the Spirit pours out life.

2 CORINTHIANS 3:5-6 TPT

Let's recognize up front that we're incapable of living this life well in our own strength. Many of us fight that idea because we feel like strong, independent women. We have solid opinions and life experiences fueling our confidence. We manage families and businesses while doing a million other things each day. But the reality is that our strength and competence come from God. They will wane with time if we go it alone. But when we ask God to give us what we need, we'll be blessed by His gracious and empowering presence in our lives.

• •

Dear God, I need You every day.
In the name of Jesus I pray. Amen.

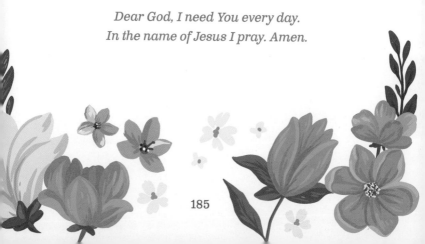

185

THE EVIDENCE OF GOD

"In previous generations he allowed the nations to pursue their own ways, yet he has never left himself without clear evidence of his goodness. For he blesses us with rain from heaven and seasons of fruitful harvests, and he nourishes us with food to meet our needs. He satisfies our lives, and euphoria fills our hearts."

ACTS 14:16–17 TPT

There is evidence of God's goodness everywhere. If you look, you can see Him in your circumstances. You can see Him in restored relationships. You can see His fingerprints in your healing and restoration. You can see His compassion as you grieve. Scripture tells us that all good things come from God, and you will be blessed when you look at your life through that lens. You are not left alone to fend for yourself. It's not up to you to make things happen. Let God be the one who satisfies you and fills your heart with hope. Open your eyes to see God's blessings in your life every day.

. . . .

Dear God, make me aware of Your presence in my life! In the name of Jesus I pray. Amen.

DEATH MEANS NOTHING

"You don't have to wait for the End. I am, right now, Resurrection and Life. The one who believes in me, even though he or she dies, will live. And everyone who lives believing in me does not ultimately die at all. Do you believe this?"
JOHN 11:25–26 MSG

For some, Jesus' message in these verses is a difficult concept to grasp because it goes against the ways of the world. For the nonbeliever, there is no hope after death. But when you have secured your faith in Jesus, death has nothing on you. Your last breath on earth leads to your first breath in heaven. You are blessed with the gift of eternal life with God. And while we can't possibly understand how wonderful it will be, we can live without fear of the future. We can rest in the beautiful truth that we will spend forever in God's presence.

• •

Dear God, thank You for the blessing of Jesus, who has secured my eternity with You. I am forever grateful! In the name of Jesus I pray. Amen.

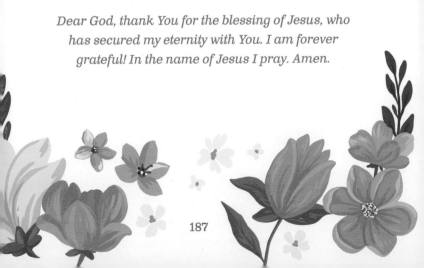

187

ETERNAL BLESSINGS

Some people store up treasures in their homes here on earth. This is a shortsighted practice—don't undertake it. Moths and rust will eat up any treasure you may store here. Thieves may break into your homes and steal your precious trinkets. . . . For where your treasure is, there your heart will be also.
MATTHEW 6:19, 21 VOICE

What a weighty challenge to keep the right perspective on your life in the here and now. What a powerful reminder to see the bigger picture of faith. Many of us collect earthly treasures, feeling blessed with big homes and new cars and whatever else may be trending. We expend time and effort to gather what makes us feel good. God's Word says this is a "shortsighted practice" because nothing from here matters in heaven. What's more, all could be lost in a moment. Fix your heart on eternity and store up blessings there.

. . . .

Dear God, I don't ever want earthly treasures to mean more to me than what's waiting in heaven. Keep my eyes focused on You. In the name of Jesus I pray. Amen.

A NEW HEART

"I will plant a new heart and new spirit inside of you. I will take out your stubborn, stony heart and give you a willing, tender heart of flesh. And I will put My Spirit inside of you and inspire you to live by My statutes and follow My laws."
EZEKIEL 36:26–27 VOICE

When we think of all the ways our hearts have been tainted by the world and hardened by our circumstances, we know that only a powerful God could exchange them for something new and good. Let that sink in. He will remove the hurts and heartaches and wash away the pain. God will undo unforgiveness. And He'll put His Spirit inside so you're able to live a faithful life. Let this bless you today as it fills you with hope for the future.

. . . .

Dear God, remove my stubborn, stony heart and give me one that's fleshy and full of love. Thank You for Your supernatural ability to bless me in such meaningful ways. In the name of Jesus I pray. Amen.

189

NEVER CEASE PRAISING

I will lift my praise above everything to You, my God and King! I will continually bless Your name forever and always. My praise will never cease—I will praise You every day; I will lift up Your name forever.
PSALM 145:1-2 VOICE

Have you ever considered that your praises are the perfect way to bless God? We see His faithfulness to reward us for obedience, but do we take time to bless Him for loving us so well? Make it a point to give God the glory. Let Him know you see all the ways He powerfully intersects your life. Give Him credit for His magnificence. Praise His name for every good thing that comes into your life. Scripture tells us to never cease an attitude of gratitude toward the King of kings! He is worthy of our praise today and forever.

· ·

Dear God, I can't find the right words to tell You the depth of my appreciation for who You are and how You bless my life. I'm in awe of Your goodness and moved by Your compassion and care. Thank You! In the name of Jesus I pray. Amen.

190

GENERATIONAL BLESSINGS

One generation after another will celebrate Your great works; they will pass on the story of Your powerful acts to their children. Your majesty and glorious splendor have captivated me; I will meditate on Your wonders, sing songs of Your worth.

PSALM 145:4–5 VOICE

You can create a generational blessing by simply passing on your story to those who are younger than you, whether your children or grandchildren, your nieces or nephews, or the kids in your neighborhood or church. Your testimony is powerful because it highlights the truth that God is alive and active in our lives. It encourages others that hope and help are possible. It teaches them to open their eyes to look for God's provision. And at the same time, it encourages your heart as you remember the stories of God's faithfulness and the blessings given to you by a loving Father.

• •

Dear God, what a privilege to help grow the faith of the next generation. Open my eyes to see opportunities to share Your goodness with others. Make me intentional to recount the times You have moved mightily in my life. In the name of Jesus I pray. Amen.

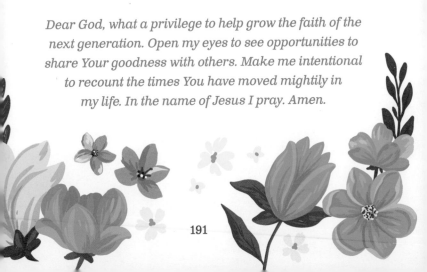

WONDERS AND POWER

*You answer our prayers with amazing wonders
and with awe-inspiring displays of power. You are
the righteous God who helps us like a father. Everyone
everywhere looks to you, for you are the confidence of
all the earth, even to the farthest islands of the sea.*

PSALM 65:5 TPT

Be blessed by the truth that God not only hears your prayers, but He answers them too. When you're hurting or need help, your Father in heaven intercedes. And His timing is always perfect. Scripture says He answers with amazing wonders. It says His displays of power are awe inspiring! Even more than that, in Him we can have confidence for resolution and restoration. Friend, you are not alone. You have a powerful God with unshakable love for you. Let Him know what you need.

*Dear God, You never settle for mediocre and I'm so
grateful. Thank You for answering prayers with such
fervor and hope. I am blessed because You always
go over and above my expectations! You're simply
magnificent! In the name of Jesus I pray. Amen.*

192